THE ALPHABET MOSAICS

Dana Redfield

Edited by Carla L. Rueckert

© 2009 L/L Research

The Alphabet Mosaics

Copyright © 2009 L/L Research

All rights reserved. No part of this book may be reproduced or used in any form or by any means—graphic, electronic or mechanical, including photocopying or information storage and retrieval systems—without written permission from the copyright holder.

ISBN-10: 0-945007-24-8
ISBN-13: 978-0-945007-24-1

Published by L/L Research
PO Box 5195
Louisville, KY 40255-0195
USA

Email: contact@llresearch.org
Web: www.llresearch.org

DEDICATION

This book is dedicated to the Light Workers of Tabernacle Earth

and

To the Tomorrow Tree.

Acknowledgements

In diverse and timely ways, many people helped me complete this project. While society might judge some kinds of help more valued than others, such as considering anything that involves the gift of money as most valuable, I cannot. For instance, when my cousin Lynn Oyler, whom I barely knew, encouraged me strongly over the telephone to complete this work, it was as helpful to me as John Andrews giving me a very good used computer when the old one crashed.

Without these kinds of help, and the ongoing encouragement of family and friends, I could not have survived to finish this work, which was started in 1993 with the curious thought, "I want to know every letter of the alphabet intimately." I could not have imagined the doors that would open, once I began this quest.

Along the way, although in no way do I mean to belittle the practical helps I received, the greatest gifts were not of the material kind. It was the love that was experienced between myself and the many other people who graced my path and helped along the way that will follow me to the Other Side. As this project began in 1993, forgive me if I've forgotten to list you here. In reality, nothing is lost or erased; everything is "recorded," everything counts, and everything is finally brought into the light, I believe.

With deep gratitude, I thank my parents, Nolan and Yvonne Morse, my brothers Paul, Mike, Tim, Steve and Phillip Morse, my sister, Sue Baldwin, and my daughter, Michelle Tomburello.

I thank my friends, Jerri Lillibridge, Dan Star, Jane and Moshe Melkior, Mary Rodwell, Martin Law, Roman Vodacek, Elihu Edelson, Carla L. Rueckert-McCarty and Jim McCarty, Frank DeMarco, Nancy Dorman, Jill Roe Bennet, Marlene King, Donna Levy, Ila Lee Swanburg, Joan Thomas, Jim Veitl, Bob Friedman, Connie and Ed Mills and Taunya Jones.

Thanks also to the many "friends of Bill W." who were such a joy and inspiration to me over the years, helping me stay strong and grateful as we "trudged the happy road of destiny" together. If I tried to name all of these friends, it would fill a whole chapter.

I am very grateful, also, to all of the people who helped me stay alive to complete this project; otherwise I could not have finished this ABC book, which was to have been delivered to Hampton Roads Publishing Company in the summer of 2003. Unfortunately, cancer interrupted this book's planned completion.

Thanks to Dr. Douglas Rock and the staff at St. Mary's Hospital in Grand Junction, Colorado. Also, thank you, Dr. Kelley, for the biopsy when it was unclear how you would be paid.

In Moab, thanks to Dr. Jonas Munger, Dr. Steve Rouzer, Dr. Jim Kempa and all of the staff and nurses, especially those special angels on earth, the hospice nurses, Anita, Connie, Nancy, Doug, Chris and Beth.

Thanks to Dr. Chris Duchet and Dr. Meic Schmidt at the Huntsman Cancer Institute in Salt Lake City. Also, thanks to the patient and compassionate people at the Utah Work Force Services, and all of the people of Utah who make possible Medicaid assistance for people like me.

Last, but hardly least, thank you, God, whom I may fathom barely through the love of Jesus Christ. Thank you Rowah, The Servants of EI, and the flower bringers!

TABLE OF CONTENTS

Preface: Journey through the Alphabet 6

Editor's Preface 12

Intuitive Overview: The Alphabet Mosaics and Concept Fields 14

How to Read the Mosaics 19
    The Mosaics 19
    Concept Fields and Letter Realms 20
    The Cipher 21
    The Number Totem Pole 22
    The House of Life 22
    Page Turners 23

Wisdoms and Letter Mosaics 24

A Biographical Note and a Note on the Typography 76

Bibliography 77

Appendix: Other Materials 80
    Alpha-Omega Man 80
    Destiny Woman 82
    Fairchild 84
    Humaniel 86
    Alphabet Tree 88
    Three Letter Charts 90
    The House of Life 94
    Crossing the T-Gate into the Arch of Infinity 96
    Hebrew Letters by Toby and Edelson 98
    Master Sheet for the Letters 100
    Set I: Five Compound Drawings 111
    Set II: Six Compound Drawings 113
    Set III: Six Compound Drawings 120
    Set IV: Drawings with Larger Concepts 127
    Set V: Abstractions 135
    Unifying Principle 141

About the Author 144

Preface: Journey through the Alphabet

> *It is a puzzle what drives one to take one's work so devilishly seriously. For whom? For oneself? One soon leaves, after all. For one's contemporaries? For posterity? No, it remains a puzzle.*[1]

Because I can no better describe my initiation into the journey through the alphabet than I did in 2000, I am including, below, this excerpt from pages six through nine of my book, *The ET-Human Link: We are the Message:*[2]

> Over the years, from the dreams of extraterrestrials, to the communications, through the catalyst, and afterward, I was always of two minds, one skeptical, logical, and analytical—the "daylight mind," which tenaciously clings to taught knowledge; the other, the part that "just knows" things, but has no words to communicate the knowing until I wrestle with angels to give voice to the mystery.
>
> It began innocently enough in August 1993, as an excitement building in me as I prepared to host a writer's workshop for a Seth Conference in Colorado. I wouldn't be talking about writing in conventional ways; instead, the focus would be on the magic of communication, which I had stumbled upon like a crystal rose left on the path by fairies.
>
> As was stated in *Summoned*[3], it began when I noticed certain correlates of letters in names and words that were meaningful to people in personal ways. For instance, the letters MO were strung like pearls on an unseen string around my life. My birth name was Moore, I was adopted by Morse, I was living on Moenkopi Street, in Moab, Utah, and my best friend's name was Montgomery. These were hints of something profound that seemed to overlay our lives like an invisible template.
>
> As I prepared my presentation for the conference, my mind was galvanized by the mystery. I hoped to show aspiring writers something of the enchanted forest of communication beyond the concrete city of language. I was seeing something of the blueprint and inner architecture of communication, a mechanics of meaning hidden within the outward structures, like seeing, in a wooden rocking chair, the tree from which it emerged.
>
> And so in a fire of excitement like nothing I had ever felt before, I whipped together charts and posters and handouts, marked up with the formulae and hieroglyphics of my discovery.
>
> I was a child discovering a new face in the mirror, a soul behind the silver shining through.
>
> By October, the presentation was a vague memory of kindergarten stuff, as I sat at my kitchen table, day and night, a student in the invisible college of communication.
>
> It was both me bringing up into the light of consciousness memories, it seemed, of a long forgotten science of language, and also angel energies attending, as if hovering over my

---

[1] Albert Einstein, *Einstein; A Portrait:* Corte Madera, CA, Pomegranate Artbooks, 1984.

[2] Dana Redfield, *The ET-Human Link: We Are the Message:* Charlottesville, VA, Hampton Roads Publishing Company, c2001.

[3] Dana Redfield, *Summoned; Encounters with Alien Intelligence:* Charlottesville, VA, Hampton Roads Publishing Company, c1999.

shoulder, instructing, guiding, inspiring. The rightness, the passion, the ecstasy I was feeling made it seem that I was born to do this work, with everything else quickly receding into a pale memory of a life spent stumbling in the shadows of the sparkling world I was penetrating at my kitchen table.

The essence of the light was discovered in the letters of our alphabet, their very lines hiding mysteries of designs and energies unseen by eyes trained to recognize only the outermost meanings taught and recorded in the dictionaries and thesauruses.

I was rediscovering the music of language and her minstrels were talking to me. The form of the genius came not as melodies on the page, but rather as a hidden design glimpsed in the numbers behind the letters. These were discovered by analyzing the geometric shapes of the letters and how each related to the others, revealing an esoteric mathematical design that I sensed underlay every created thing on Earth. I had studied quantum physics, and the geometry of fractals was speaking to me. Like Benoit Mandlebrot, who discovered the mirror world of fractals, I was seeing, in the glimmer of language, the art forms of the letters generating pictures in the conscious mind that translated to meanings in the subconscious beyond the reach of the intellect.

As a cloud cannot be captured and studied under the lens of a microscope, it was impossible to record on paper everything I was seeing in the door of light between two worlds. The complex letter and number formulae were but chicken scratchings on the ground compared to the vision in my mind. The complexity evolved into drawings that captured the essence of concepts too large to be contained in words. Sometimes I felt a force moving my hand to draw at a level of artistry beyond my normal abilities. It all made for a suspicion in the minds of observers that I had cracked my beam and gone over the edge.

But I knew it was not so. I discovered I was not alone in knowing about the hidden design in language. A friend, Magda MacIver, recognized in my work a similarity to Kabbalah, an ancient and esoteric system of teaching practiced by Jewish mystics. Ordering a couple of books on the subject, I confirmed that, indeed, my work resembled that of Jewish mystics. And some of the stories emerging from my work with letters and numbers were Jewish in tone and flavor, persuading me to believe that the ease and familiarity that had attended me at the table was suggestive that I had done this work before in a past life.

The above was written approximately three years before I contracted with Hampton Roads Publishing Company to write *Alphabetech and Contact: Tools for Revolution of Mind, Life and Spirit*. Ten years of working with the letters had not made it any easier to imagine a product that might appeal to other seekers, but finally I managed to write a proposal that passed muster, and I was offered the contract in February 2002.

The trouble with making proposals and contracts for creative products is that creation has its own mind and is not subject to time constrictions. Soon after the contract was signed, the idea of the Mosaics presented itself to me, and the longer and deeper I worked with the letter Mosaics, the more clear it became that the Mosaics would be the heart of the book. There was no way I could have made a proposal to create the Mosaics, as the idea did not communicate itself to me until after the papers were signed.

And then came the unplanned event of illness. In 2003 there were signs of cancer in my right lung. Having no insurance, and not qualifying for charity at the local hospital, I did what I could for myself. I began a fierce health program that included quitting smoking. I had been a heavy smoker for 40 years. I didn't think I could quit. But with the help of God, as I understand God, and guides and angels, I succeeded in tapering down to 0 smokes per day in 10 months.

I felt fairly healthy then, and hoped that the flashy spot on the x-ray wasn't cancer after all. But I had another sign of it in July 2003. Because I had stopped smoking, I felt I could press for help, and I got it. A CT scan and a biopsy showed that there was a slow-growing tumor in my right lung.

I was already past deadline for the *Alphabetech* book, but that was the least of my problems. Radiation treatments were recommended and I agreed. This meant a 234-mile round trip by automobile from Moab, Utah, where I lived, to St. Mary's Hospital in Grand Junction, Colorado, 5 days a week for 8 weeks. St. Mary's was the radiation treatment facility closest to Moab. St. Mary's is a charity hospital, so I was able to get help while the slow wheels of Social Security Disability, and Medicaid turned, finally qualifying me for financial assistance three months after treatments began.

In December 2003 I was declared free of cancer, but the exhaustion of radiation kept me working on the Mosaics at a much slower pace, and as the days, months and years passed, it became increasingly clear that the end product was going to be much less than I had bargained to create in 2002 when I signed the contract.

It also became clear that the smaller book was going to be the better book, because it became something I am passing on to you, the readers, to work with, to use for inspiration and as tools to expand your consciousness.

Ironically, I am exerting myself to write these pieces of the book, the Preface, the Introduction and so forth, all the while knowing that the less I say about the Mosaics, the better. Because they are designed by Spirit to serve as tools for your journey, not mine. I am simply functioning as Spirit's scribe. My journey is nearly done, in this body-personality. And what a journey it has been!

This is a good place to encourage you, the reader, to listen carefully to your own inner guidance as to whether or not these Alphabet Mosaics will be helpful tools for you. While the Mosaics are not creations of Kabbalah, there are similarities enough that I want to caution you.

Kabbalah is ancient and its secrets are closely guarded. In the Jewish Talmud there is a famous story of four scholars who embarked upon the path that is called Kabbalah today. The four scholars were overwhelmed with experiences. Cooper says, "… one [scholar] died, one became demented, one gave up his faith, and only one, Rabbi Akiva, survived unharmed."[4]

It didn't surprise me to learn that the general attitude in Judaism is that to pursue mystical wisdom is a dangerous proposition. I was quick to understand in some deep way that I was working in fields and realms that could result in mental imbalance and who knew what other dangers. At times, I *was* overwhelmed.

But I wasn't in that much danger, really, because I had no intent to gain mystical wisdom or secrets. I was following my heart, and it was made clear to me early on that I was guided and protected.

---

[4] Rabbi David A. Cooper, *God is a Verb: Kabbalah and the Practice of Mystical Judaism:* New York, Riverhead Books, 1997, p. 169.

I never felt I was doing a work that would "change the world" or anything so grandiose. Nevertheless, I respected the gift of all that was being shown to me, and I felt I should make an effort to share it with others. That turned out to be a daunting task. But it fits, too, my feeling that it was all mostly a personal journey, and as such, not much of it could be shared.

And that is the beauty of the Mosaics: they are not definitive markers on a map to expanded consciousness, but "fingers pointing," a rather vague wave of the hand—what you seek is over there—somewhere. And this is in keeping with the great tradition that honors the path of the individual. While we share collective archetypes, and all is/are connected, we are each as unique as snowflakes.

Imagine the letters of the alphabet as realms we pass through in our journey through life. The linear progression, A-Z, 1-26, helps for order and organization in the brain, but of course letters are in essence larger than life, and cannot be forced into set patterns. Words are proof of that. Like life, letters are lived in the words and experiences that compose creation in the making.

One of the gifts of working with the letters, and the numbers they represent was that I came to respect and see the genius behind form and organization. As a wild-eyed creative artist and poet in my youth, I was of a mind to throw off all of the constrictions of forms and rules. The inner pull to individuate was particularly strong in me and rebellion was the weary road I would naturally take before I realized that life was way more mysterious than I had imagined.

Any true journey will come to a place/event/time where old ideas will be shattered. This is represented in my "House of Life," found in the Mosaics and Appendix, as a catalyst about three-quarters of the way up the structure. How we respond to the life-changing catalysts will determine the golden years of our life—the maturity and integrity one can gain if the ego is not so inflated as to end the life there at the challenge, either in death or in an increasing number of failed attempts to try and force one's narcissistic beliefs upon the world. Inevitably there will be another catalyst, if the ego survives the first, life being designed to help guide us toward resolution and freedom.

In the Tarot deck, the Tower card and the Wheel of Fortune card illustrate the idea of the catalyst in "The House of Life" drawing. As the journey progresses through the alphabet from A to Z, keep in mind that this is a rudimentary exploration of the concept fields and realms within the linear order as a mental guideline, like the rope and harness the mountain climber is wise to use.

I hope that, if you are a fellow quester who finds appeal in this journey through the alphabet, that the Mosaics will serve as a centering device at those times when you feel lost, confused or afraid. It's not the "knowledge" in the Mosaics that is important, but paradoxically it is what emerges in the spaces around the images and words that will be your find—something to calm or inspire, something to restore faith that you/me/we are here for a purpose, and that no matter how rough the going, you/me/we will find our way, and in the end won't regret the soul investment in this arduously difficult world.

Imagine consciousness as a map to use as you find your way across the untamed land- and ocean-scapes of Earth, and as you seek the shining bodies in the sky you hope to explore. Like conditions on Earth and in the sky, our consciousness is constantly undergoing changes. Nothing is fixed; everything is in flux. But these bodies and brains are brilliantly designed to allow for focus, in order to carry out our purposes, known and hidden, in the human becoming story.

Preface: Journey through the Alphabet

In *The ET-Human Link*, I wrote about human life on Earth as composing three stories: the belonging story, the gathering story, and the becoming story. I hoped to make clear in that book that for me the contact and encounters experienced were part of the fabric of my whole life, though admittedly the awakening process was at times shocking. But if a person, or a people, were to undergo an expansion of consciousness, couldn't we logically expect some surprises and shocks?

And that is the rub, of course—the argument as to the true nature of the ET/contact/encounter phenomenon. As an experiencer and as a writer, it was made clear that my task was to do my best to understand the mysteries of my own experiences, and to communicate these to others in hopes of helping to reduce the fear that is only natural when we are faced with something new.

The good news is that although experience that defies age-encrusted beliefs can be shocking or frightening, through courage we begin to develop the precious gift of discernment, particularly in recognizing the difference between beliefs and truths.

This Preface is not meant to expand on discussions about the ET-UFO phenomena, except to make it clear that my sudden interest in the alphabet in 1993 turned out to be the key that would open the doors through which I needed to go in coming to terms with these changes in my life. I apologize for being so vague about it here, but I did write two books to share my experiences and thoughts on the subject, and it would be impossible to summarize in a paragraph, or even a page, the depths I was able to explore in the writing of those books.

It is also impossible to write to any depth of my experiences in exploring the alphabet over the past 14 years. The Mosaics are a kind of summary of my journey, but of course words, spoken or written, no matter how artfully rendered, are not substitutes for experience. The purpose for creating the Mosaics was to leave a kind of map of my experiences for any who would feel the pull to journey, using the letters as guides, into unexplored realms of consciousness.

There is so much more to be said about the Alphabet Mosaics, but I will have to leave it to others to say. After the lung cancer was healed, a different kind of cancer came up in my kidney and spread to the spine before the surgeon removed the kidney. After a very painful operation to remove a chunk of bone from my spine, the cancer still spread, and there was no medical way of stopping it.

After the shock faded, I resolved to finish the Mosaics as thoroughly as I could, and I am amazed that I've been able to do this much in such a short time. Family, friends, doctors, nurses and hospice workers have all helped me enormously so that I could assemble the parts of the book that will survive me, the body-personality-shell. And that will satisfy my soul and Spirit that I did all I could to preserve the letters, the symbols for the energies that make the words that create our world. (Word + L = World.)

Below is a message that came to me on May 8, 2005. I was writing about the roots of Kabbalah. I don't recall the context, but it found its way up through the piles of papers to belong in this Preface:

> Now, if I look to religion—my own Judaic roots—then the door to my creativity shall shut. I will have to bow to religion. The religion has all been worked out. Surely, Rabbis and others continue to think with the Torah as the hub in the wheel of their thoughts. But in the purest concept of Kabbalah, the wisdom is in the letters, which are ever-changing, you see, and with words that come, forming the knowledge and wisdom that guide our walk at any given time/space.

This means that at any given space/time, we can go back into the letters to find new knowledge to guide us. And does not wisdom guide us to do this, from time to time? All knowledge becomes brittle after it has been handled too much—manhandled by the manipulators, by those who are selling it as a product.

"Knowledge is power." When you hear this, it is like chimes in the mind of those who have ears. In the words, between the letters and all around the words, there is a sound of shattering. The vessel that has been the container for the knowledge that has guided your way has cracked and will soon explode as if by the thunder of God's voice, uttering a new Word. The shards of the vessel scatter like seeds blown by the winds of autumn. Winter comes like death in a cold white cape, arms out wide over the whole world.

If any of the seeds would live, we think they will grow into freakish, distorted forms with no souls, children of the thunderous rage that broke the vessel and scattered the pieces like useless millet. But spring does come, like an unexpected bride, to awaken man who has forgotten his wedding vows in the hibernation of the pain of his loss of understanding. Like a goddess who touches with a wand of golden light, spring lights on man, giving him rise, showing him again the way of life.

And so it is that we are all keepers of the seed and the faith that sees us from age to age, and world to world. Such is the awe that we feel, dying and living again, in a becoming story no one knows until it is lived.

Dana Redfield
May 10, 2007

Editor's Preface

I first corresponded with Dana Redfield using the postal service in the long-ago days of the eighties, before either of us had internet access. Dana loved *The Law of One* series and she and I became friends as we discussed it. In the nineties, when we had both achieved e-mail competency, our correspondence flourished electronically.

Dana appreciated the way I "heard" her. I have been a researcher of the UFO contactee phenomena since the seventies, so the wide range of her contactee experiences did not cause me to see her as anything other than the quite normal and lovely, albeit unique, person that she was. She felt comfortable with me in a way that was hard for her to find among most of those around her, simply because I felt comfortable with her.

She and I shared a mystical Christianity, loving Jesus with all our hearts and being touched often by the Holy Spirit. Our bond was always deepest on Christmas Eve, when we would e-mail each other one word: Jesus.

I watched Dana from afar as she moved to be with one she loved, coming home again to Moab sadder and wiser. Later, I watched her again attempt to form a settled relationship, this time with a volunteer here at L/L Research. Again, she returned to Moab. Her fortune with maintaining the usual man-woman relationships was never as good as her spectacular gift for achieving contact and rapport with unseen beings and essences.

I was with her across the e-mail miles as she sat at her kitchen table for hours on end, day after day and year after year, drinking in the alphabet and all it had to teach her. I watched the Mosaics come through many versions before her final work was done on them. I know first-hand that for all its slenderness, this present volume is the result of an enormous amount of her dedicated study, research, meditation and channeled insight.

And I witnessed her gallant struggle to stave off her physical ending long enough to get this book, in its present form, to L/L Research.

Editing Dana Redfield's writing was interesting and sometimes challenging. Her personal shorthand did not always translate into written English. What I have changed of her introductory text and the text of her appendices is largely a matter of punctuation.

Once in a while I found oddities, such as the ten pages during which she typed "1" instead of "I" when referring to herself. I was tempted to leave such things as they were, charmed by the depth of her whimsy. In the end, I followed her specific instructions to me and brought them into common usage.

I have not touched one iota of the Mosaics and the Wisdoms! This was also per her instructions.

I want to thank Roman Vodacek, who scanned the manuscript so that it could be edited and then printed, and who worked with me to assemble the manuscript.

Thanks also go to Ian Jaffray, who generously helped me with the final tidying-up of this unusual manuscript and making it ready for printing. His artistry is responsible for creating the front and back cover art from Dana's drawings. Thank-you also, Michele Matossian, for working with Ian to conceive of the conversion of the front and back cover Mosaics into the look of tablets.

And I wish to thank Melissa Black, who re-drew Dana's "Master Sheet" for the Appendix, using a magnifying glass, strong sunlight and infinite patience to winkle out the original words, which in many cases were illegible to the naked eye. She also re-inked a faded column of the second page in the part of the Appendix called "Letter Charts" to restore it to legibility.

It has been my privilege and pleasure to ready this manuscript for print. Reader, enjoy this little book! Lose yourself in its highways and byways! And celebrate with me the "desert rose" and wonderful soul who collaborated with Spirit to bring it to life.

Carla L. Rueckert
Louisville, Kentucky
April 13, 2009

Intuitive Overview: The Alphabet Mosaics and Concept Fields

> *There is not a word or even so much as a letter of what the Holy One has given that does not contain precious mysteries.*[5]

What is a concept field? It is the name of each letter Mosaic. It describes a relationship between symbol and meaning. More than a name or one-word descriptor, a concept field represents a field or range of related ideas within the realm of a particular letter.

In our present world, letters are commonly viewed as abstract symbols, devoid of meaning. Today, words hold the meaning, with the letters as mere components. But in truth, each letter has a rich history of meaning. In the beginning, the letter was the meaning. The letter was a picture, such as the image of an ox head (A).

Viewing the symbols up the left side of Mosaic page "A," you can see the progression from ox-head to the Modern English A. Ox-head was not merely a word or name for an animal. The symbol or picture of the ox-head brings to mind a field of related ideas. In my opinion, in some ways, the history of written language is a history of evolving human consciousness.

In the mythological pre-Tower-of-Babel times, the Bible (New International Version) says,

> "Now the whole world had one language and a common speech."[6] and, "… the whole earth was of one language."[7]

The text goes on,

> "But the Lord came down to see the city and the tower that the men were building. The Lord said, 'If as one people speaking the same language they have begun to do this, then nothing they plan to do will be impossible for them. Come, let us go down and confuse their language so they will not understand each other.' So the Lord scattered them from there over all the earth, and they stopped building the city. That is why it was called Babel-because there the Lord confused the language of the whole world. From there the Lord scattered them over the face of the whole earth."[8]

In this story, I read a reference to a time of great change that can only be perceived from a higher viewpoint, such as the timeless God-view. When we are caught up in the drama of radical changes such as are occurring today, it is difficult, if not impossible, for even the sagest among us to predict the world coming to be as a result of the multidimensional changes in progress.

For instance, we know that computers and cell phones are changing the world. We know that wars are changing the world. We know that changes in the climate are changing the world. And

---

[5] Lawrence Kushner, *Honey from the Rock; an Introduction to Jewish Mysticism:* Woodstock, VT, Jewish Lights Publishing, c2000, p. 12. *(Zohar III 174b)*

[6] *The Holy Bible*, Genesis 11:1 (New International Version).

[7] idem (King James Version).

[8] *The Holy Bible,* Genesis 11: 5-9 (New International Version).

these are only three visible changes. Other changes happening in less visible ways count as much, but probably can only be assessed in the future, looking back, or from the God-view, above time.

Today there seems to be a collective agreement that we are in a cauldron of great change. I believe we are at a threshold of radical changes and that this is affecting human consciousness, and, naturally, the way we communicate.

In *God is a Verb,* Rabbi Cooper says,

> "According to Jewish mysticism, five thousand seven hundred fifty-five years ago, a new paradigm of human consciousness was born. It was a paradigm shift in the world, for it was a level of awareness that could consciously merge with its own origin. The beginning and continuation of this merging make up what we call the process of enlightenment. Kabbalists say that we are rapidly approaching another major paradigm shift in awareness. It will be called messianic consciousness, and we will understand everything in an entirely new light."[9]

I believe the story about the Tower of Babel is a legend speaking to the last major shift in human consciousness. In language, the shift from pictographs such as Ox Head, House and Camel to the abstractions, A, B and C used in words that often have multiple and changing meanings signifies a major change in the way people thought and communicated.

In ancient times, "writing" was not so easy as this, words flowing on a shaving of wood (a piece of paper), or sentences flowing across the monitor screen like sky writing on glass. From brain to hands to chips to screen to printer—presto! Information foments, usually more than we wanted to know; too much for any brain to absorb in a day.

In ancient times, when scribes etched on stone or scratched symbols on laboriously prepared dried animal hides, parchment or papyrus, symbols had to signify a lot more. They did not have the luxury of assembling multiples of words, as is the custom today. Communication became more externalized, complicated and complex, like a magic tool that could be used for good or evil by individuals seeking power over the many—politicians, religious leaders, educators, attorneys, advertisers. Anyone can use language to deceive.

And this is why, I believe, today there is a lot of talk about "getting real" and getting in touch with our feelings, or talking and writing from the heart. There is much more awareness today of the pitfalls of intellectualism and the limits of reason and logic.

While hourly, weekly, monthly, annual "world news" presents us with the pretentious tedium of "business as usual" harking back to King Solomon's lament that there is nothing new under the sun,[10] the artists, visionaries, seers and thinkers with uncommon sense are still and always among us, and persistently "carrying the message" in multiple ways that appeal to the multiple diversities in education, intelligence, consciousness and preference.

The wording, and even the details, differ from one mind and group to another, but if you are reading this, you probably are aware that we are on the brink, and in the midst, of a major course change.

---

[9] Rabbi David A. Cooper, *God is a Verb: Kabbalah and the Practice of Mystical Judaism:* New York, Riverhead Books, 1997, p. 1.

[10] *The Holy Bible,* Ecclesiastes 1:9, "What has been will be again, what has been done will be done again; there is nothing new under the sun." (New International Version)

Some call it the "end of days."[11]

Others describe it as a transformation of consciousness.[12]

Others speak of a shift from Third Density to Fourth or Fifth Density.[13]

According to Jose Arguelles' view as explicated in *The Mayan Factor*,[14] the end of this age will happen in December 2012.

And in the Seneca world-view, we are between the "Fourth World of Separation" and the "Fifth World of Illumination"[15]

Some of the information above appears as "jots" within *The Alphabet Mosaics*, like dots on a map of a world too vast and complex for me to see like a land, though it is a metaphor that works for me, speaking of consciousness and intelligence.

As I experienced the depths of each letter realm, I could only hope that the images on the Mosaic pages would adequately represent the rivers of meanings coursing through the books that I used as references to help bring focus.

For instance, in the concept field of "ages,"[16] it is hoped that Noah's ark and the image of the modem communication tower, with its aerial piercing the heavens, will work to convey, as "information art," one age coming to an end as another age begins.

In the spirit of the timeless tale of the Tower of Babel, "age" changes mean changes in time-place-space and communication. Moving through the Mosaics, the messages communicated are expressly unique to each letter. But it is the same message, in essence, in multiple presentations.

If it were a message that could be written out here in words, there would have been no call for this book. Precisely because we are in the midst of changes that are, and will be, affecting the communication centers in our brains, this book is a kind of bridge and primer for changes in consciousness greater than can be described in words, as we presently think we know words.

A, B, C, D—Archer, Book, Chalice, Diamond—the concept fields served to focus my mind to create the particular stories and maps the Mosaics make. One can play with the concept fields. Imagine the images on the B Mosaic page, for instance, if the concept were Butterfly instead of Book. On the M page, if Mountain were the concept field, how might the Mosaic differ from Moon as the focus?

---

[11] This term is often used within both Judaism and fundamental Christianity.

[12] This phrase is used by Carl Johan Calleman in his book, *The Mayan Calendar and the Transformation of Consciousness*, and is also used by many other New Age sources.

[13] *The Law of One, Books I through V,* and many other New Age and channeling sources as well, contain channeling suggesting a movement from Third to Fourth Density. Lyssa Royal and many other New Age and channeling sources suggest instead that we are moving into Fifth Density.

[14] Jose Arguelles, *The Mayan Factor; Path Beyond Technology:* Santa Fe, NM, Bear Publishing, c1987.

[15] Jamie Sams and Twylah Nitsch, *Other Council Fires Were Here Before Ours : a Classic Native American Creation Story:* San Francisco CA, Harper, 1991.

[16] This is a sub-field within the Mosaic for "A," which has an overall concept field of "Archer."

Intuitive Overview: The Alphabet Mosaics and Concept Fields

In one experiment, I drew each letter to fill a whole page, and then used it as a tool to enter a meditative zone that was in nature A-like, or G-like, or S-like in energy. Once while meditating on one of the letters—I forget which—I had a sudden vision of a blue flame that seemed motionless, but I knew it represented a reality beyond our 3D world. I felt blessed by the vision.

After working with the letters, over time, my whole consciousness about words changed. Words became like windows into other realms of awareness, and doorways into deeper understandings. I believe that all of the work I did helped to break the literally spell-binding effect that words can have on the brain. The more I worked with the letters as symbols, the less susceptible I was to the spellbinding effects of words, and the more discerning I became of everything I read.

I think, too, that working with the letters and numbers outside the kingdom of words with fixed meanings serves to bring into better balance the right and left hemispheres of the brain. But experience cannot be taught. Words don't transfer experience from one brain to another, which means that ironically all you can do is "take my word for it."

What worldly knowledge there is in this book can be found in many places, but there are not many places where you can go to learn how to acquire knowledge that is of the wellspring of living waters, a wellspring which is uncontaminated and unrestricted by the dictates which hold sway in the spellbound kingdom of words. In this sense, I am saying that the function that is called "guidance from the Holy Spirit" could be understood as a function of the brain.

I am not suggesting that religion is nothing more than myth and superstition, and science is reality. In my mind, religion and science are different ways of perceiving reality. People pursuing either religion or science can become spellbound by the words they consider to be the truth, whether that truth is claimed to have come from God or to have been proven to be true by the rules of science.

Imagination, intuition, synchronicities—these have contributed to great discoveries as much as the legwork of gathering facts and following the strictest of scientific protocols. More importantly, strengthening whole-brain thinking/feeling can help us as we are, and where we live. Most of us are not going to make giant discoveries for humankind, but all lives are enriched, I believe, by each individual's effort to expand consciousness and strengthen his whole-brain thinking/feeling.

I believe that much of the fervor and passion of religious fundamentalist beliefs are rooted in unawareness of the power of words on the mind. The same can be said of any kind of dogma, be it religious, political, academic or scientific. We all know that words are powerful, yet many intelligent people express total bewilderment as to why various extremists, usually of a religious following, would persist in beliefs that appear to be blatantly and obviously untrue to any but the believers.

I can't explain it myself, but I do believe that anyone who seriously considers *each letter of each word* in any statement, Biblical or otherwise, cannot become spellbound by words—cannot fall victim to extreme interpretations of words. Because when one acquires awareness of letters and words as *symbols,* one can never again be hostage to them as realities, in and of themselves.

In other words, from my journey through the alphabet, and through the gift of coming to know each letter intimately, in my heart, I consider human worship of words to be a form of insanity or, in a religious context, a form of idolatry.

Personally speaking, my journey through the alphabet was a quest to know God—as I understand God—better. This has happened like the ancient Kabbalah mystics said it would happen—in the white spaces around the letters, where one experiences freedom from any kind of mental bondage to words. There is no way to explain the knowing that comes in the white spaces. It has to be experienced.

Paradoxically, the less that the spelling of words held power over my mind, the holier that words became for me. This happened because I saw letters as "guides"-in the sense of the guidance and teachings of the Holy Spirit.

I hope this intuitive overview has helped to clarify the meanings and purposes of these Alphabet Mosaics. But if the whole of this book could have been conveyed in words alone, there would have been no need for art, image and symbol to compose a large part of the communication.

And if it were a simple message to convey, there would not be a need for 26 Mosaics.

The hope and intent is that the meaning will be imparted, Mosaic by Mosaic, with the sayings and concept field commentaries to help guide, but not shape, the thoughts, as that is each person's gift to find and express, uniquely and privately.

Perhaps we are on the brink of conscious thought-form construction. Perhaps communication as we have known and experienced—from Ox-Head (A) to Weapons in the Sky (Z)-were a kindergarten in a School of Evolving Consciousness. Is this an idea too fantastic and overwhelming, to relax the thinking mind and take in the images of a Mosaic that is a favorite letter? I rest best in the realm of Q-who knows why? Questions, questions … and so the thinking person's quest.

Love and Light,

Dana Redfield
Moab, Utah
February 12, 2007

How to Read the Mosaics

The Mosaics

Up the left side of each Mosaic are glyphs highlighting the history of the symbols from Egyptian to Modern English. *The World Book Encyclopedia* was my main source for the letter symbols. Other sources used for comparison, such as Nigel Penwick's *Magical Alphabets*, are listed in the Bibliography.

Certain letters, such as M, still clearly resemble the original ancient Egyptian symbol. Other letters have changed significantly over the ages. In the Appendices are charts that show the progression of all of the letters of the alphabet from Egyptian to Modern English.

Above each totem pole of glyphs is the concept field with its symbol, name and cipher equivalent. We will discuss the concept fields and letter realms below. The symbols for each letter, shown in the concept field circle, emerged early in the work, in the autumn of 1993. I viewed all of them as three-dimensional, geometric objects. Many hours were spent studying the myriad relationships between all of the letters, as triangles, squares, circles, half-circles, ellipses, spheres and ovals.

In the body of each Mosaic, at the top is a pictorial gallery of my vision of the unique nature and energy of each letter. Words and pictures work together in the Mosaics as both information art and as one person's expressed understanding of the complex meanings in the background of each of the letters that compose the words that spill out of our mouths and from our hands in the course of the amazing, shared event we call communication.

The upper, middle and bottom tiers of the Mosaics were not strictly designed, but patterns emerged as I worked. In the upper tier, something of the relationship of shape and energy is conveyed. In the middle tier, the body of the letter, the elemental nature and quality of the each letter is expressed in art drama, as the drama of our lives reveals much about human nature. In the lower tier is a kind of summary or story, depicting the essence of each letter.

During the process of creating the Mosaics, I wasn't thinking in terms used here to try and describe the finished pages. None of these "insights" directed the work.

For each letter, I first perused the *American Heritage Dictionary* and *World Book Encyclopedia* to get a feel for the essence of each letter in the world of words. This was years after I'd already immersed myself in the quest to know each of the letters intimately.

The analytical work of perusing dictionary and encyclopedia before creating the Mosaics brought to my attention certain distinctions of each letter not noticed before. I learned, for example, there are an inordinate number of trees with names beginning in Y, such as the Yew Tree, yet Y may be the slimmest section in the dictionary. Since the name Yew Tree for Y was an intuitive selection in 1993, discovering that academically Y was much about trees affirmed the work I'd done.

As I worked to complete the Mosaics over the months and years, many similar kinds of discoveries strengthened my sense that the letters were more than the meaningless nuts and bolts of words.

Concept Fields and Letter Realms

More than a name such as Archer, Book or Chalice, a concept field represents a field of related ideas within each letter realm. The names just came to me, but I gave them thought over the years. Each name was "tested" when I came to make the Mosaics. Most of the original names passed muster, but a few changed.

For instance, in the beginning I chose Ianus for the letter I-a variation of the name of the Roman God Janus, who could see both ways-past and future-a double-faced fellow. The name of the month January comes from Janus. The idea behind the god-name Ianus seemed so "r" in essence, I was reluctant to let it go, but I also felt it was a cop-out in a way to use someone else's name.

In the process of selecting a name for I, I probably learned more about the nature of a concept field than I did working with any other letter. For instance, the picture and symbols that came to mind when I was thinking "Innkeeper" was the name were very different than what came to mind when I began to work with the name "Integrator."

And it became clear to me that my work with all of the Mosaics in the wholeness called the alphabet revealed things about individual letters that were not seen, looking at them one letter at a time. When I delved deeper into the realm on I, a special connection between I and N (Navigator) and O (Orchestrator) was revealed. Then it was like the original experience I had with each letter: I did not choose the name so much as the names came to me as the best descriptors of each. But several, I and W, for instance, were slow in revealing their natures to me. Curiously, I is the last letter of the cipher arrangement, and W is the first.

The concept field directs a particular focus, and the names best reflect the essence or nature of each letter. A letter realm is a kind of landscape. It might seem at first glance that all of the words in A's letter realm begin with A; words of the B realm begin with B; and so on. For the most part this is true. Organization of words by the first letters is a way to make order.

But as is true for any reality in our world, appearances deceive. For example, the word "babble," which has the same root as "baby," is more B in nature than the word "belief." The root of the word belief is "leubh-," the same as for the word love. Technically then, "belief" belongs on the L landscape; but I would have had to work for another 14 years if I'd wanted to be so precise as to sort words by their roots, rather than by first letters. Just as is impossible to know where beach and ocean begin and end, letter landscapes overlap and intermingle.

Another example: consider the words conform, deform, form, perform and reform. The core word "form" is of the F realm, but cousin words are all over the alphabet. Then take words whose core word is "port"—apportion, comport, deport, important, proportion, report, rapport, support and transport. Again the core word is of the P realm, but cousin words are found throughout the alphabet.

When I want to check out a family of words based on core words such as port or form, I mentally consider the letters most commonly used for prefixes: A, C, D, E, I, P, R, T and S.

Another example is in the J Mosaic. Within the concept field of Journeyer is the idea of a trajectory, a course the journeyer might follow. Jugglers around the House symbol helped to illustrate the family of "ject" words. There is the "subjective" Jagged Path. There is the "objective" of the journey. The "trajectory" is perhaps a "projection" in the minds of the jugglers. (Other "ject" words such as adjective, eject, inject and reject were not used in this illustration.)

It is even more complicated to consider all of the words that include "ect," as in correct and elect, as a vast group on some Word Tree too complex for me to imagine in detail. But it is worth the mention to better illustrate what is meant by "the essence of the letter," and where words may belong in fields and realms. Take away the "ect" from the "ject" in the words listed above and what remains? J! like a beacon flashing-here is pure "J-ness." But for the sake of order, sub-j-ective will show in the S landscape; ob-j-ective in the O landscape, and so forth.

The Cipher

The Cipher is a tool that I believe was given to me. I was inspired to do certain work that revealed a different arrangement of the alphabet. That arrangement is:

WZGXVLYQCKHPUMENJOFTSRBDAI

Technically, the cipher arrangement isn't the alphabet. In Greek, Alpha is A and Beta is B; in Hebrew it is Alef-Bait. Using the first two letters in Greek, the alphabet would be called the Double-Upsilonyod. Using the first two letters of the Semitic alphabet, it would called the Wah or Vauyod.

I used the cipher for Gematria, though when I started, I did not know this was the name for the exercise, nor did I know of its ancient roots. In *God is a Verb*, Rabbi Cooper says,

> "… each letter of the Hebrew alphabet has a numeric value. The first letter, Aleph, has the value of one; the second letter Bet, the value of two; and so on."[17]

In the ancient Kabbalah tradition, each letter has a set value, such as 1 for Aleph and 400 for Tau. In my cipher, the values are from 1 to 26, and the alphabet begins with W (1) and ends in I (26).

Before the cipher emerged, I did a great deal of work in cross-referencing the letters in numerous imaginative charts and graphs, all in the spirit of the quest to know each letter intimately. As is true for people, a letter alone and by itself is meaningless. It is in the nature of its connections and interrelationships that meanings take shape, and continually change.

Acting on my urges from one exploration to the next, I felt that there was a more primal order to the letters than shows in the modem A-Z, or the traditional Aleph to Tau, or Greek Alpha to Omega, order. It was a very involved process, "rating" each letter, giving each a "score" (particular values), to determine the "new order" (the cipher, above.)

In other words, it did not happen from whim or impulse. A lot of work revealed the order. And after applying the numerical values of 1-26 (W-l) to names and words meaningful to me, I came to feel that the work of revealing the cipher was inspired; because how could I have "created" such a thing, having no idea what it would reveal, when I put it to use, applying Gematria?

But it is important to say here that the revelations were subjective and personal to me. Using the cipher as a tool to explore, for instance, I discovered that my name, Dana Redfield, has the same numeric value as *Ezekiel's Chariot*, the name of my first published novel.

---

[17] David A Cooper, *God is a Verb,* op cit, pp. 52-53.

I made a huge chart with numbers up to 684. On line 149 (for example) are words meaningful to me: Los Angeles, where I was born, and Moab, Utah, where I was then living, and still do. Also on line 149 are the words "white rose," "harmonize" and "golden dawn."

Another reason I felt that creating the cipher was inspired was the fact that when I spent time applying it, usually it would work to alter my mind (or brain). In this state, often I would feel the probe of a "messenger." In other words, working with the cipher worked to alter my mind/brain in such a way as to facilitate "contact" or "channeling." I had no idea this would happen. Like everything else I did with the alphabet over the years, it was all in the spirit of the quest to know each letter intimately.

In the beginning, I was an innocent. I knew nothing about Kabbalah and very little about related esoteric practices. From the start, when I worked with letters and numbers, I experienced something like the opening of gateways in my mind. Then I had to learn to take very seriously the lessons of discernment. In these states of mind, I was conversant with beings of other orders; or perhaps it was all the expressions of the "higher self."

However, at times, the communications were clearly "two-way" conversations. I did not mean for this section about the cipher to become a discussion of the controversial subject of contact and channeling, but these experiences were the result of my use of the cipher in the ancient tradition of Gematria, and I would be remiss not to tell you—or warn you—of what can happen, using such tools.

The cipher is included on several Mosaics; X and Y to name two; and at the site of each concept-field sphere are the cipher and number equivalents. W is 23 in the alphabet, 1 in the cipher; Z, 26 in the ABC arrangement, 2 in the cipher, etc. The cipher also shows in whole on the "Tree of Life" page in the Appendices.

The Number Totem Pole

Another gift of my efforts was a version of numbers in their primal shapes. This is also shown on the "Tree of Life" page in the Appendices, and is expressed on several Mosaic pages, such as T and X.

A kind of story came to me along with the shapes that were revealed for numbers 1 through 10. If I am able (time is of the essence), I will include in the appendices the originals, which were drawn and hand-written.

(Editor's Note: I have not found this "kind of story.")

The House of Life

I dreamt about the House of Life before I discovered that my work was drawing me into the realms of ancient Kabbalah. The House is a version of the Tree of Life, in a way. I worked with it. It revealed to me four paths through life: Right, Left, Center, and Jagged. In the images of the House that appear in the Mosaics, the jagged path is emphasized.

In the Appendices, the drawing "Universal Woman" expands on the meanings inherent in The House. It is a story of life—not "the" story of life, but one interpretation of life pathways. The story is basically that there are four approaches. The jagged path touches on all paths, and knows the way around the Catalyst, which is in the uppermost tier, directly under the "attic" area.

The dot in the center of the attic area means that the journeyer has completed his tour of lives and will be moving on to higher densities. The story in The House also shows that those who get caught in the catalyst and don't emerge to complete the mission will be returning for another, or more, lives. The catalyst could symbolize materialism or any number of life challenges.

Page Turners

Last—just for fun, in the lower left hand corner of each Mosaic is a word that announces the upcoming letter. My rule was that the word had to use the letter of the present Mosaic, and the Mosaic coming up. I chose "able" for A going into B, and "conundrum" for C going into D. The word should reflect something about the essence of both letters.

Wisdoms and Letter Mosaics

A - ARCHER

Aspiration and action
are the architecture
of the Astral—
as above, so below.
The archetypical Archer
aims the arrow of intent
at the rarefied air over the arc of ages
to be actualized at Z, Zodiac.
Don't bother to analyze.
Art is the abstract language
of the Soul.
Here we are again at alpha—
another New Age.
No self-assembly required.
Be not afraid,
ancestors and angels say—
a great adventure awaits!

B – BOOK

Birds, bees, babies;
blood, bones, butterflies.
Believe it, B is about biology.
Behind everything,
even the human body and brain,
is a blueprint from the Book of Life.
In the balance,
building blocks are not all there is
to the human being.
The "busy bee" may miss the beauty
and the bliss.
Let there be breath in your banter.
Between every letter of every word
is a spacious manor.

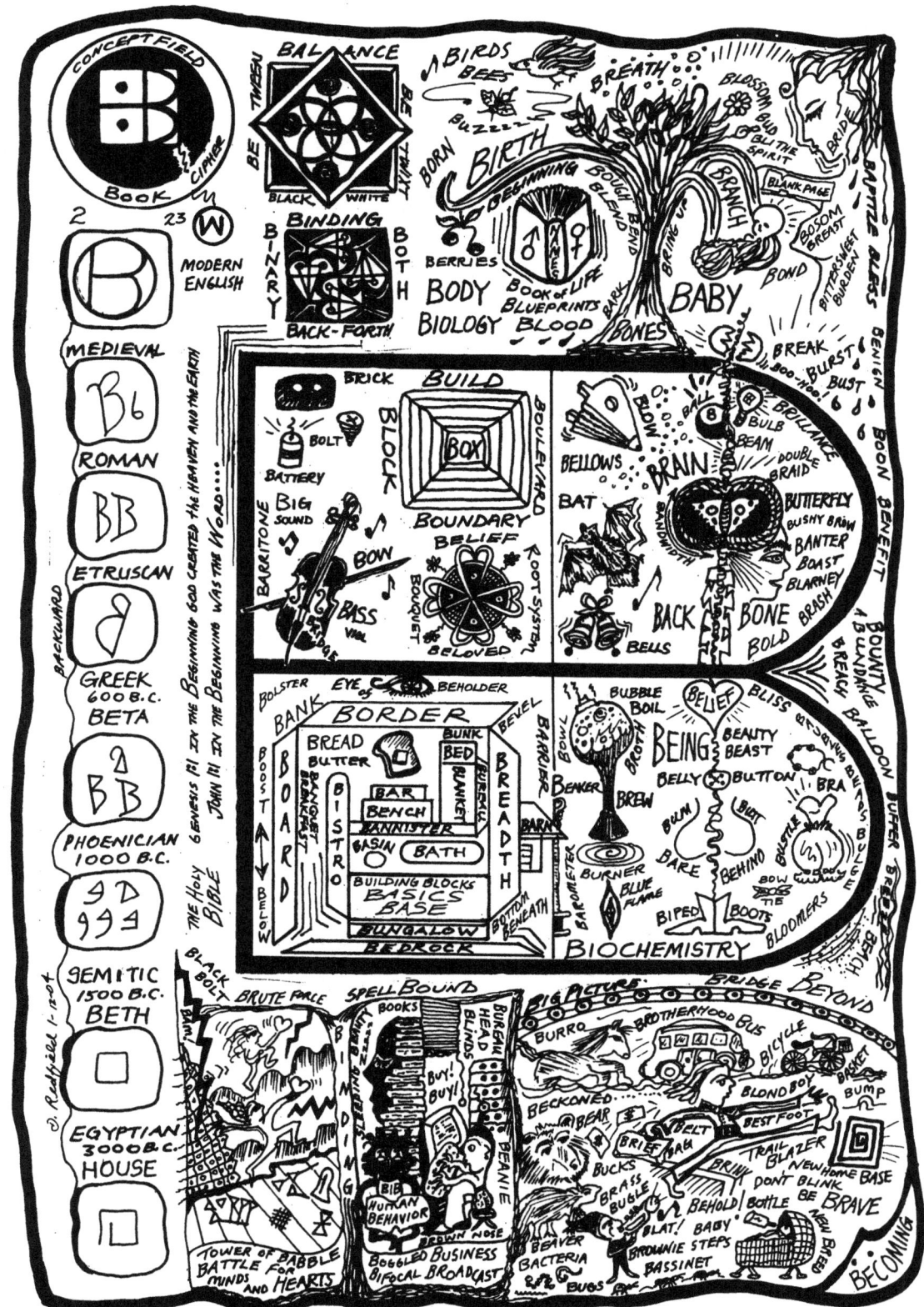

C – CHALICE

The Chalice reminds
that at this level of consciousness,
we are incapable of comprehending
the core of creation.
One's character counts more
than the combined choices of a culture.
The Hebrew camel traveled
from Egypt to Greece
and gimel became gamma.
Don't be confused;
cities, countries and even constellations
come and go,
but in the Cosmic drama,
one child is more cherished
than a whole civilization.

KHRONOS - TIME
(CHRONOLOGY)

CABALA
QBL — TO RECEIVE
ROOT

PINEAL GLAND
IS PINE-CONE SHAPE

AJNA CHAKRA
COMMAND WHEEL
(ENERGY)
PG 119
LOST SECRETS
OF THE
SACRED ARK
LAURENCE GARDNER
PG 121 -
DOUBLE - SERPENT
CADUCEUS OF HERMES
INSIGNIA OF
AMERICAN, BRITISH,
AUSTRALIAN
MEDICAL ASSOCIATIONS

A CHILD SHALL LEAD

D. REDFIELD
1/29/02
5/31/03
1-05-04
09

D – DIAMOND

Between dreams and destiny
are doorways of discovery.
Neither darkness nor death
can dissuade the indwelling Spirit;
we are all diamonds in the rough,
part of the Great Design.
Discernment is a dynamic key.
Dare to delve
into hidden dimensions.
Do or die? Big drum roll!
Determination and devotion
cannot be denied.

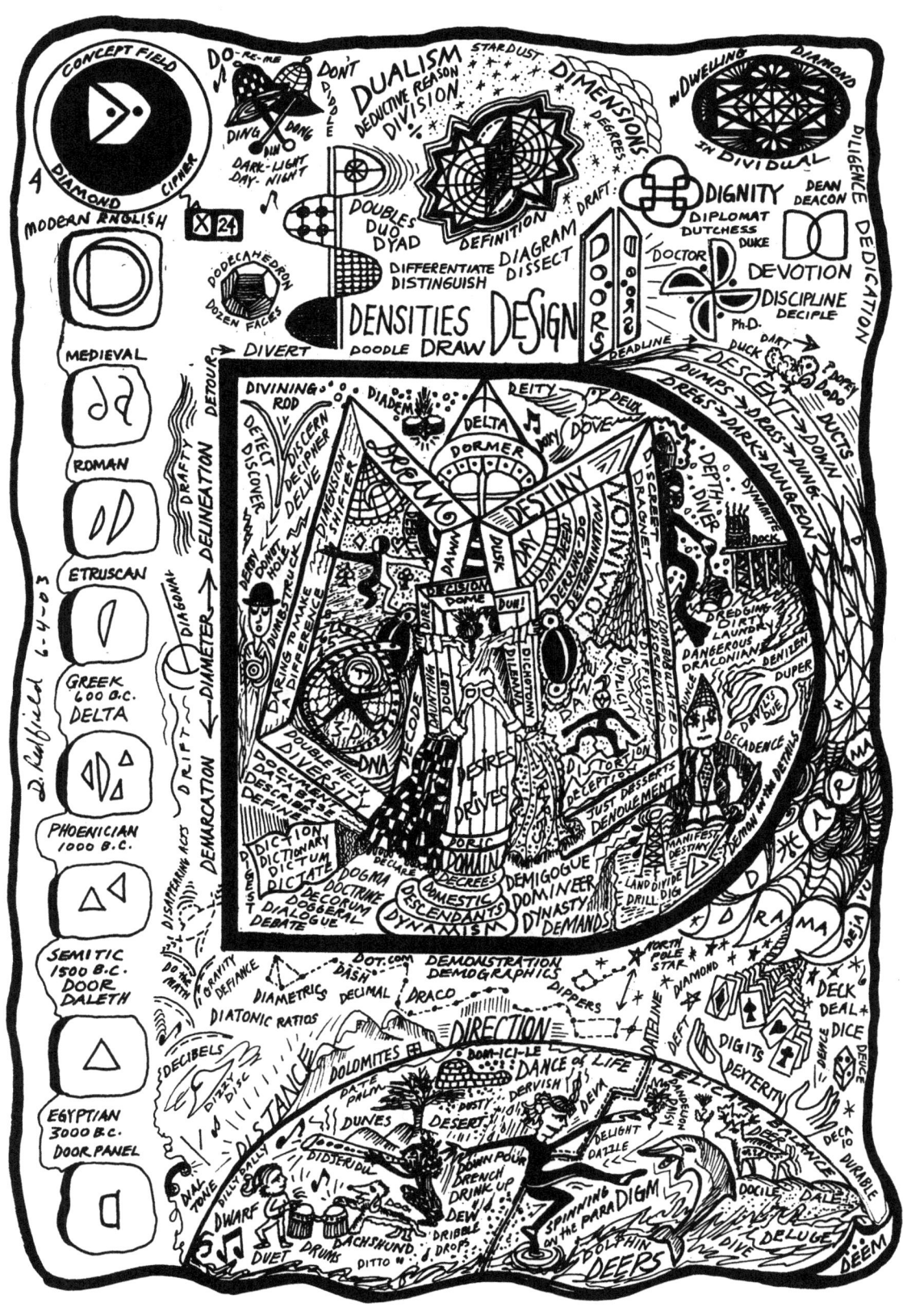

PARADIGM
ROOT DEIK
DEIKNUNAI — TO SHOW (GREEK)

DOXY - OPINION - DEK -)
PARADOX)

DHARMA — TO DO WITH INDIA AGES —
SEE Pgs 79 and 309 in
HAMLET'S MILL by GIORGIO DE SANTILLANA
(BIBLIOGRAPHY) and HERTHA VON DECHEND

D. REDFIELD
5-6-02
6-4-03

E - EARTH

Do you know Earth?
Consult your heart.
The letters and the energies
are the same—
earthheart:
where one ends, the other begins.
Elegance is the essence of equilibrium,
everything in balance,
from enzymes to emotions;
from ego to ethos.
In the ethers, the Elders watch
as we evolve over eons and epochs.
At the eleventh hour,
the steward emerges in his element,
enchanted student
of Eagle and Elephant.

F - FLAME

From feathers to firesticks,
nothing is fixed;
all is in flux,
like a flower unfolding.
Around the fabled Tree of Life,
Cherabim swinging flaming swords
protect the foundational forms
and frameworks
from destructive forces.
Now the fledgling is free
to face the future,
with the inner Flame
safe within the fortress
of faith.

G – GATEKEEPER

Round and round
globe and cycles go;
if not for Gaia and her goad,
the uninitiated might think
all is grist for the grinding mill,
nothing more.
Feet firmly grounded in our being,
eyes on the stars,
the Gatekeeper stands
between Flame and Heart,
guarding the golden child
gestating in our genes.
The gallant graduate
never expected greetings
from Galactic gawkers.
Thank goodness the Gatekeeper
is standing guard.

H - HEART

Heart-T (Trumpet) = hear.
We are the ears and heralds of Earth, here
to heal and harmonize.
Humanity's journey through history
has been half joy, half horrific,
as if Heaven and Hell
were mirrors hewed
in the hemispheres
inside our heads.
When the Heart's harp is tuned
to the harmonics of the wisdom
of the High Priestess
in the mind,
all is well
in the House of Life.

1 - INTEGRATOR

The individual may seem
to be insignificant,
mere instrument
for institutions that war
against the innovations of Spirit.
Integrator, Orchestrator and Navigator
joined to instill sacred power
in the tiny ion—
greater than the highest ivory tower.
If true, imagine the infinite possibilities.
The Information Age
is mere interlude
before Illumination.
Just an idea?
Or truth inscribed deep inside.

J – JOURNEYER

Under the jaundiced eye
of Jove,
the juvenile jumps
for the moon.
The seasoned journeyer knows
we must collect the Keys
and climb the Ladder
before we can ascend.
Juggler, jester, joker and jouster
will help us find our way
on the Jagged Path.
When our jobs are done,
we return to the joy whence we came. Tune
your ears—
the jongleur will lead you
past your fears.

K - KEYS

The quest for the keys
to the kingdom
begins and ends within.
Knowledge and experience
go hand in hand, like kith and kin.
To gain wisdom,
become a kid again,
keen to the kinetic energy
of Kokopelli
and the kaleidoscopic eyes of Owl.
What's the use of having keys
if the doors they open
are unknown?
Knock, ask —
know thyself.

L - LADDER

Up the ladder we ascend,
lessons to learn,
that's life.
If we always color
inside the lines
and adhere to the letters of the law,
we might succeed in the world
but may lack in lightness
in love and laughter.
Language is the paradoxical obstacle
to luminescence.
Left brain, right brain,
fishes and loaves—
don't get lost in the labyrinth
of lofty logos.
Life is simpler and purer
closer to the lotus.

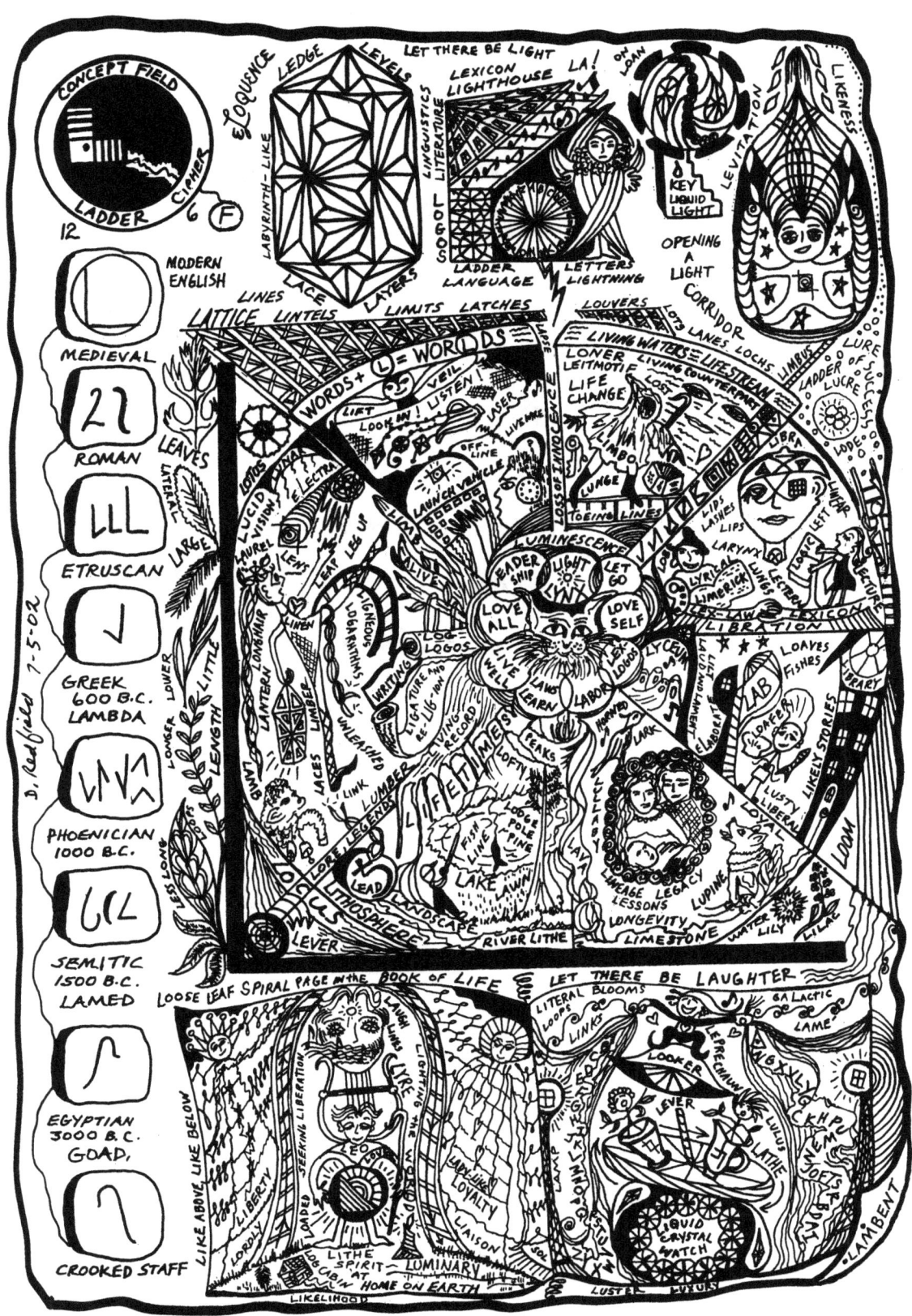

M - MOON

Mind over matter,
so say the metaphysicians.
Metamorphosis over mortality.
Mother Nature has her maps
and her mechanisms,
her measures and her meanings
for every movement,
including e-motions.
From microbes and molecules
to mountains and the Milky Way,
the mystery of life eludes.
Up comes Moon—
magic maker
shining in the night.

N - NAVIGATOR

The novice Cosmonaut
must learn the names,
numbers and notes
of all the nicks,
nodes and narratives of time,
night and netherworlds.
Someone has to know
how to navigate
the waters of the dark
so that the next Noah
in his cosmic ark
can help to rescue
Mother Nature
for the next
age.

NECESSITA' NON HABET LEGEM
NECESSITY HAS (OR KNOWS) NO LAW

THE HARPER DICTIONARY OF FOREIGN TERMS
EDITOR, EUGENE EHRLICH

D. Redfield
7-26-02

O – ORCHESTRATOR

Sometimes
on the edge of sleep
we may hear the chimes
of the sacred pipe organ,
sounds of the inner Orchestrator
collaborating with Navigator
to wake us to a higher octave
of consciousness.
Like Jonah of old,
we might be reluctant
to obey the call
from the Higher Order.
Three days inside
the belly of a whale
will make a believer
out of any
one.

P - PROFESSOR

To listen to the Professor,
a Pollyanna might think
P to be the primary power
behind the alphabet—
more precisely
the human mouth pontificating
on the principle of the thing.
Meanwhile, the prodigy points
at the Pleiades and prophesies
about our purpose in life
while Pan from his perch
plucks and smiles,
perceiving all
to be a passion play
to prepare the human psyche
for passage
to higher
or parallel planes.

Q - QUESTER

Minding Ps and Qs
and a high I.Q.
barely prepare the seeker
for the adventure
of the vision quest
and the quickening
of the quantum leap.
In the Egyptian glyph
is a monkey—
monk and key?—
but the Hebrews speak
of the voice of the angel calling.
Who's to quibble?
Answers to questions,
queries and quandaries
are found in quietude.

R - RAINBOW

From the realm of Rainbow
flow the color rays
from red to ultra-violet
for the enrichment of the human race,
and all of the resources
for which we are responsible.
Too much reliance
on reason and rectitude
can make the Rivers of Life run dry.
Rhythm, rhyme and romance
are part of the dance.
The rainmaker from the Silver Ray
will show us how
to ride the waves
until we are ready for reunion
with loved ones
on the other side.

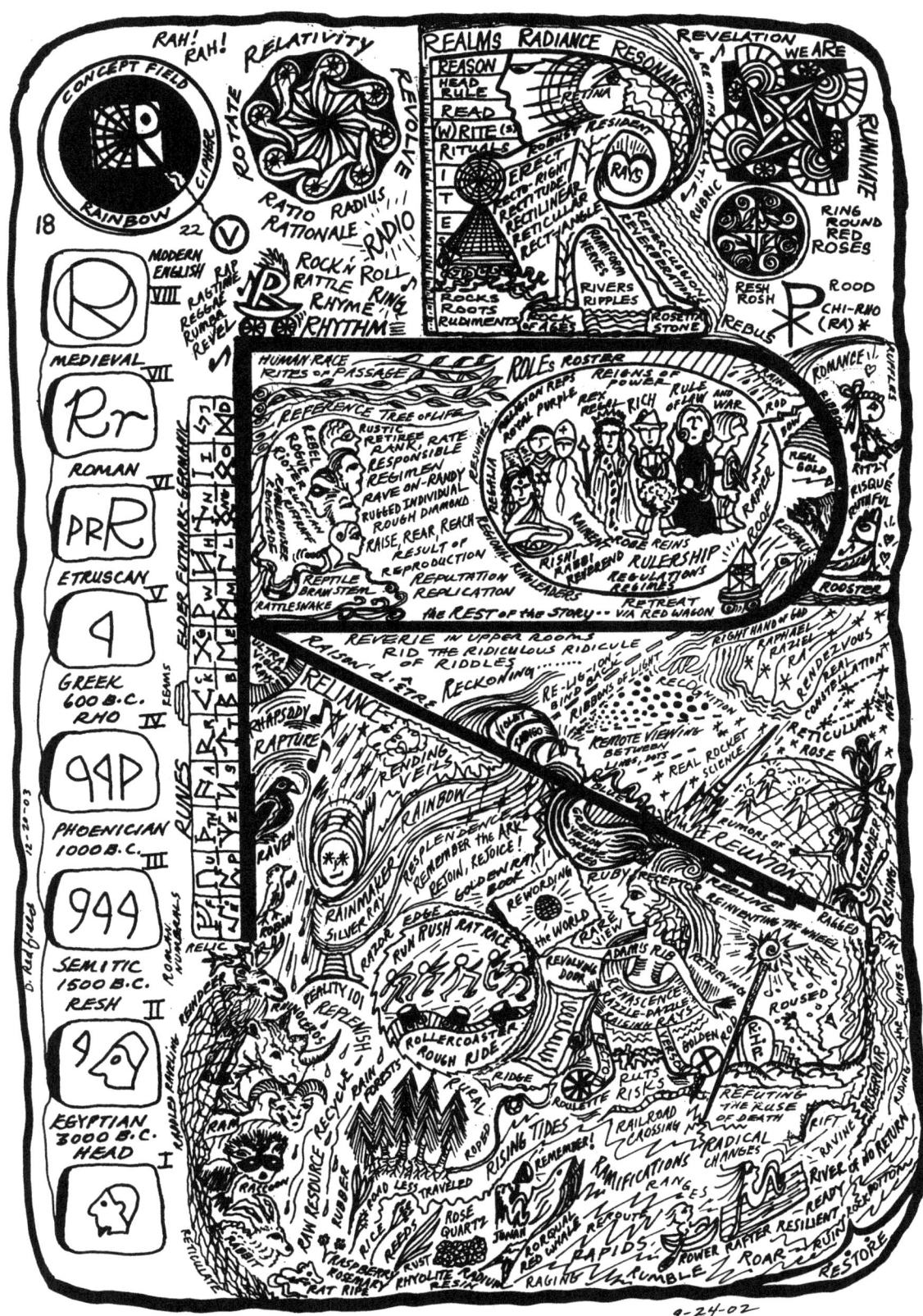

Rosetta Stone
Jean Charles Champollion

RAISON d'ÊTRE
REASON FOR BEING
REASON FOR EXISTENCE

RELIGION – RELIGIO (GK)
RE-LIG–
ROOT MEANS: TO BIND BACK
(LIGAMENTS, LEGS....)

* CHI-RHO
GREEK CHRISTIAN SYMBOL
FORMERLY "SUN GOD" – RA
(SON —— RAY)

RESH-ROSH: HEAD

9-24-02
D. REDFIELD
10-14-02
RE-VISION
5-8-03
12-20-03

S - SUN-STAR

Light and sound vibrations
from sun and stars
sustain us through seasons
and stages
up through the ages
from the Sphinx
to the science of the spirit
in a spacecraft
bound for Sirius.
For now such stellar splendors
must wait for us
to complete the schooling
of our sixth and seventh
senses.
The spellbound mind
finds release
in the sacred silence.

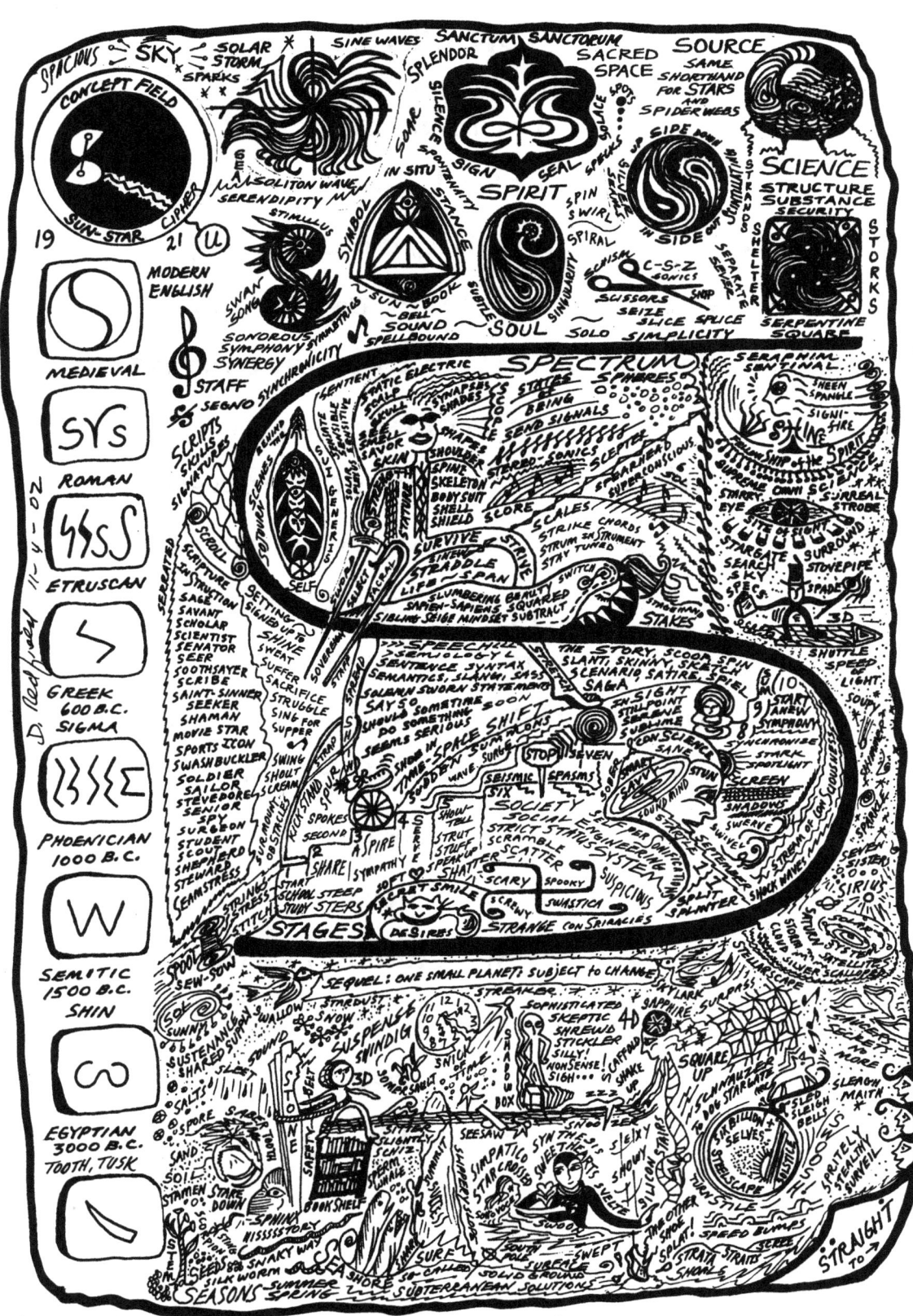

T - TRUMPET

In ancient times,
T was the last letter,
tacitly a turning, or cross-point.
Twentieth of twenty-six today,
Trumpet heralds transformation
in time to take stock
of what it is we most treasure.
Technological triumphs
making possible travel
to Tau Ceti may tantalize,
but nothing quite trumps
the beauty of trees
or the tranquility
of "trust thine own truth."
Tomorrow, "tele-thought"
may suddenly be
as common
as talk.

THOR - NORSE GOD OF FORCES
(AND THUNDER)
THURSDAY IS THOR'S DAY
TUESDAY - OLD NORSE TRYSDAG
(BRIGHT SHINING GOD)

D. REDFIELD
11-26-02

U - UMBRELLA

Though U,
Like Double-U, F and Y,
stemmed from V, Vau,
Like you and I,
each letter is a unique creation.
Even so,
we are all expressions of one—
Uni-Verse—verb unfolding.
From the severing
of the umbilical cord
to our ultimate destination,
we live under the Umbrella
that symbolizes separation
between the collective conscious
and unconscious.
The heart knows
what the mind
cannot understand.

V - VEIL

The provocative voices
of our ancestors
down the vines and vectors of time
bear witness to the vistas
and visions of our destiny unfolding.
To avoid the tyranny
of mental overload,
it is advisable to retreat
behind the Veil
to the sanctuary
in virtual reality
where the Vestal Virgins
restore vitality.
Then, revitalized,
we can fulfill our vows
to thwart violence
and exercise valor
and vigilance
to the end.

VOX POPULI – VOICE OF THE PEOPLE
VOLANS – FLYING FISH CONSTELLATION
VOLANT – FLYING
VØ·EKT△ – JOY ETERNAL
VIMANA – HINDU "UFO" (SKY VEHICLE)

VISHNU – "LION MAN"
pg. 117
THE MYTHIC IMAGE
Joseph Campbell

1-13-03
D. Redfield

W – WISEMAN

Word + L = World.
We can wonder
if Double-U emerged
to work wonders
where wrongs have warped
the lighted way to wisdom,
well-being and wholeness.
The wonder child and whiz kid
work together
within and outside the Web of Life
to clear the world of illusions
and restore harmony to waters,
woodlands and winds.
When "I will" and "we will"
finally wed,
the Wiseman appears
to wash away
our tears.

X - THE NAMELESS ONE

X is the crux, and ex- is past,
and what is next,
or exed out of existence,
for all we know. X is at the center
of nexus and axis,
and is the mystery behind the Sphinx
and the Phoenix.
X is the unknown X-factor
and the unnamed Planet X.
Names as we know them
may be exclusive to the Explicate Order—
all that is exterior and external,
the comfort zone of xenophobic skeptics
who scoff at the story
of extraterrestrials
xylophoning
home.

Y - YEW TREE

Y is the yield of yarns,
myths and ancient yore,
something your hand (yod) can grasp,
like the mystical Archer's bow,
hewn of the physical Yew Tree.
Rooted in reality,
yin and yang,
the mythical Tree of Life
keeps on giving
through cycles, yugas and Great Years,
thanks to yet-to-be understood
celestial mechanics.
Beyond the Yellow Ray
the light is green,
beckoning us toward
the Tomorrow Tree.

YUCATEC YEAR COUNT
THE MAYAN FACTOR
JOSÉ ARGÜELLES

YAXCHE –
YUCATEC TREE OF LIFE
LOST KINGDOM OF THE MAYA
GENE S. STUART
GEORGE E. STUART

YĀNA –
SANSKRIT –
"WAY" IN BUDDHISM

(HINDU)
YONI – WOMB, VULVA

COLOR RAYS –
"TREE OF MIND"
THE RA MATERIAL
ELKINS, RUECKERT, McCARTY

YANTRA –
MEDITATION AID
DICTIONARY OF SYMBOLISM
HANS BIEDERMANN

YUGAS –
THE MYTHIC IMAGE
JOSEPH CAMPBELL

YAHRZEIT
JUDAIC CANDLE
LIGHTING CEREMONY –
MEMORIAL

YGGDRASIL –
NORDIC LIFE TREE

YESOD –
FOUNDATION

YLEM –
ETHEREAL
LIFE SUBSTANCE

YEHIDAH – (5TH SOUL LEVEL)
GOD IS A VERB
RABBI DAVID A. COOPER

D. REDFIELD
3-27-03

Z - ZODIAC

Under
the mighty Zodiac,
a person, a mere zoion,
can feel awfully small,
almost zero, zilch, nothing at all.
By day the stars
are hidden from our gaze;
by night we doze,
Zzzzzz—perchance to dream
of zealous children of the new age
storing the letters A-Z
in a secret ark,
like a time capsule for the heart.
From ox head/A
to weapons in the sky/Z,
the Archer zinged the arrow Zayin
across the ages
to find us here,
contemplating the seals.

A Biographical Note and a Note on the Typography

Elihu Edelson, who designed the text pages facing the Mosaics, was born on March 30, 1925, a day he shares with two of his favorite artists—Francisco Jose de Goya and Vincent Willem Van Gogh. A veteran of World War II and a graduate of the University of Florida, he has worked in the arts as critic, educator, painter, and calligrapher. He is also the publisher of the spiritual magazine quarterly *Both Sides Now* (http://bothsidesnow.info.)

Aside from his work on his magazine, this is Edelson's first venture into major typographic design.

The text pages opposite the Mosaics are typeset in a calligraphic font called Carolingia, designed by William Boyd. Its name is derived from the Carolingian manuscript book hand developed by Alcuin of York in the ninth century at the behest of Charlemagne (Carolus Magnus). It was the first hand to use both capitals and small letters together. Up to that time all manuscripts were written in what we would call capitals, or technically majuscules.

What Alcuin did was to employ earlier Roman letters for the caps, while a transitional hand, called half-uncial, was adapted for the small letters (minuscules). On examination it can be seen that Boyd pulled off some sleight of hand himself, if one will pardon the pun. His capitals are based on uncials of about the sixth century CE, while the small letters derive from half-uncials from about the eighth century. Thus the Carolingia font can be used for uncial, half-uncial, and Carolingian texts.

The only catch is that authentic Carolingian writing was slightly slanted, whereas half-uncial was not. However, for the purposes of this book, a perpendicular style looks better for the symmetrical layout, so we thank Boyd for his clever adaptations.

BIBLIOGRAPHY

General Reference

American Heritage Dictionary of the English Language, William Morris, Editor: Boston, Houghton Mifflin Company, 1980.

Bartlett, John, *Bartlett's Familiar Quotations, Fifteenth and 125th Anniversary Edition*, edited by Emily Morison Beck: Boston and Toronto, Little, Brown and Company, 1855, 2005.

Cosmic Connections, by the Editors of Time-Life Books; *Mysteries of the Unknown Series*: Alexandria, VA, Time-Life Books, c1988.

Biedermann, Hans, *Dictionary of Symbolism, Cultural Icons and the Meanings Behind Them*: New York, NY, Oxford—Facts on File, 1989, 1992.

Harper Atlas of World History: New York, Harper Collins, 1986.

Harper Dictionary of Foreign Terms, Revised and Edited by Eugene Ehrlich: New York, Harper & Row, 1987.

Holy Bible, King James Version: Ballantine—Ivy Books, New York, 1991.

Holy Bible, New International Version: Peabody, MA, The Zondervan Corp., 1984.

Random House Dictionary of the English Language, Second Edition Unabridged, Stuart

Berg Flexner, Editor in Chief; Leonore Crary Hauck, Managing Editor: New York, Random House, 1987.

World Book Encyclopedia: Chicago, IL, Field Enterprises Educational Corp., 1967.

Other Sources

Arguelles, Jose, *The Mayan Factor: Path Beyond Technology*: Santa Fe, NM, Bear & Company, 1987.

Armstrong, Karen, *A History of God*: New York, Alfred A. Knopf, 1993.

Briggs, John & F. David Peat, *The Turbulent Mirror*: New York, Harper & Row, 1989.

Campbell, Joseph, *The Mythic Image*: Princeton, NJ, Princeton University Press, 1974.

Carroll, Lewis, *The Adventures of Alice in Wonderland*: Mount Vernon, NY, Peter Pauper Press, 1940.

Case, Paul Foster, *The Tarot: A Key to the Wisdom of the Ages*: Richmond, VA, Macoy Publishing and Masonic Supply Co., Inc., 1947, 1975.

Cooper, David A., *God is a Verb: Kabbalah and the Practice of Mystical Judaism*: New York, Riverhead Books, 1997.

De Santillana, Giorgio & Hertha Von Dechend, *Hamlet's Mill, A Nonpareil Book*: Boston, MA, David R. Godine, Publisher, 1998.

Ereira, Alan, *The Elder Brothers: a Lost South American People and Their Message about the Fate of the Earth:* New York, Alfred A. Knopf, 1992.

BIBLIOGRAPHY

Elkington, David, with Paul Howard Ellson: *In the Name of the Gods:* Sherborne, England, Green Man Press, 2001.

Einstein, A Portrait: Quotations: Petaluma, CA, Pomegranate Artbooks, 1984.

Elkins, Don, Carla L. Rueckert and James Allen McCarty, *The Ra Material* and *the Law of One Books:* Atglen, PA, Whitford Press, 1984.

Friedman, Norman, *Bridging Science & Spirit:* St. Louis, MO, Living Lake Books, 1990.

Gallant, Roy A., *The Constellations:* New York, Four Winds Press, 1991.

Gardner, Laurence, *Lost Secrets of the Sacred Ark:* London, Harper Collins, 2003.

Hamilton, Edith, *Mythology:* New York, New American Library, 1969.

Hancock, Graham, *Fingerprints of the Gods:* New York, Three Rivers Press, 1995.

Hancock, Graham, *Heaven's Mirror: Quest for the Lost Civilization:* New York, Crown Publishers, Inc., 1998.

Hancock, Graham, *Underworld: Flooded Kingdoms of the Ice Age*: London, Penguin Books, 2003.

Heinlein, Robert A., *Stranger in a Strange Land:* New York, Ace Books, 1961, 1987.

Hurtak, J.J., *The Book of Knowledge, The Keys of Enoch*: Los Gatos, CA, The Academy for Future Science, 1987.

Halevi, Z'ev ben Shimon: *Kabbalah, Tradition of Hidden Knowledge:* Thames & Hudson, New York, 1979, Warren Kenton

Jung, C.G., Edited by Aniela Jaffe, *Memories, Dreams, Reflection*: New York, Vintage Books Edition, Random House, 1989.

Knight, Christopher & Robert Lomas, *Uriel's Machine*: Gloucester, MA, Fair Winds Press, 2001.

Kushner, Lawrence, *The Book of Letters, a Mystical Alef-bait*: Woodstock, VT, Jewish Lights Publishing, 1990.

Kushner, Lawrence: *Honey from the Rock:* Jewish Lights Publishing, Woodstock, VE, 1992.

Melchizedek, Drunvalo, *The Ancient Secret of the Flower of Life, Volumes 1 and 2*: Flagstaff, AZ, Light Technology Publishing, 1998.

Narby, Jeremy, *The Cosmic Serpent, DNA and the Origins of Knowledge*: New York, Jeremy P. Tarcher/Putnam, 1998.

O'Brien, Christian and Barbara Joy, *The Shining Ones*: Kemble, Cirencester, England, Dianthus Publishing Limited, 1988.

Patterson, Alex, *Field Guide to Rock Art Symbols of the Greater Southwest*: Boulder, CO, Johnson Books, 1992.

Pennick, Nigel, *Magical Alphabets*: York Beach, MA, Samuel Weiser, Inc., 1992.

Rey, H.A., *The Stars:* Boston, Houghton Mifflin Company, 1976.

Sams, Jamie & Twylah Nitsch, *Other Council Fires Were Here Before Ours, A Classic Native American Creation Story as Retold by a Seneca Elder, Twylah Nitsch, and Her Granddaughter, Jamie Sams*: New York, Harper Collins, 1991.

Sitchin, Zecharia, *Divine Encounters, A Guide to Visions, Angels, and Other Emissaries*: New York, Avon Books, 1995.

Sitchin, Zecharia, *The Cosmic Code: Book VI of The Earth Chronicles*: New York, Avon Books, 1998.

Vallee, Jacques, *Passport to Magonia: From Folklore to Flying Saucers*: Chicago, IL, Henry Regnery Company, 1969.

Wasserman, James, *Art and Symbols of the Occult:* Rochester, VT, Destiny Books, 1993.

West, John Anthony, *Serpent in the Sky, The High Wisdom of Ancient Egypt:* Wheaton, IL, Quest Books, Theosophical Publishing House, 1993.

Wolf, Fred Alan, *Star Wave, Mind, Consciousness, and Quantum Physics*: New York, Collier Books, Macmillan Publishing Company, 1984.

Williams, David, *A Naturalist's Guide to Canyon Country*: Helena, MT, Falcon Publishing Inc., 2002.

Appendix: Other Materials

Alpha-Omega Man

This drawing reveals a hint that the original letters served as symbolic guideposts signifying the development of human consciousness, similar to variations of the Hebrew Tree of Life. The meanings of the beginning letters, A through G (including the F-U-V-W-Y family) seem to correspond to the lower chakras in the human body.

Across the middle part of the body, corresponding to the solar plexus chakra, are

- I, J, K—Hand and Cupped Hand,
- H—Knotted Rope (or window),
- L—Goad, Z—Arrow,
- with N—Snake and
- M—Water representing a transition to fourth and fifth densities (or the Heart Chakra).

E—Man Rejoicing and Q—Monkey—or "the voice of an angel calling" may represent a turning point or an awakening to a new level of consciousness beyond the lessons about control and power represented in the solar plexus chakra.

The following complete what I sense to be a hidden story behind the Alphabet:

- P—Mouth, (communication)
- S—Tooth (catalysts),
- O—Eye (appearances and judgments),
- R—Head (reasoning), T—Mark or Cross (gateways), and
- X—Fish.

X, as the last letter in this story, may signify the sign of the Age of Pisces passing, or the end of this phase of human development.

Appendix: Other materials

Alpha-Omega Man

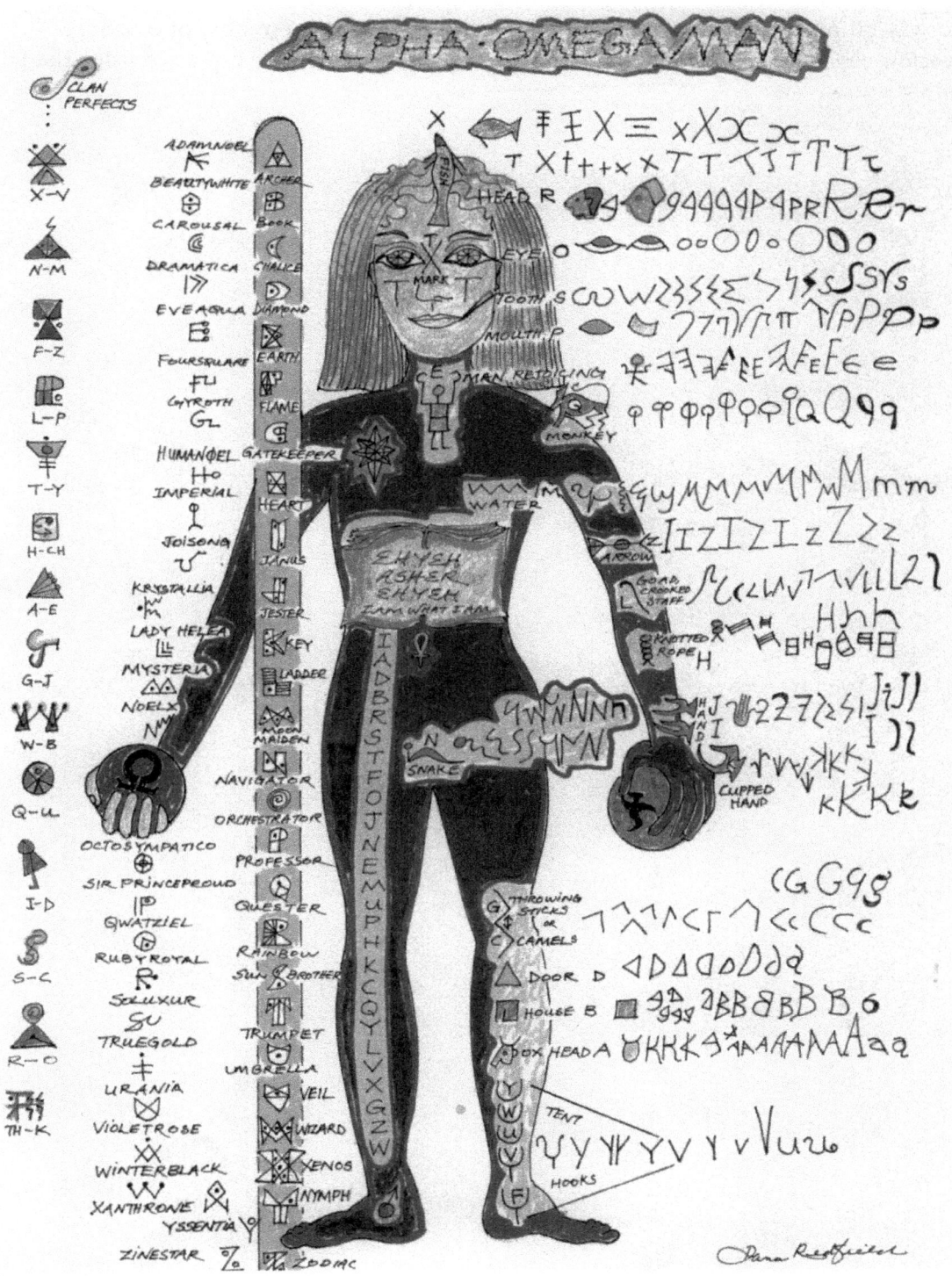

Destiny Woman

This drawing is a representation of the "House of Life," a symbol about which I dreamt. It was a doorway for much study and understanding. The drawing tells the story of evolving consciousness. Like the Hebrew "Tree of Life," many stories can be expressed using the House of Life structure.

Appendix: Other materials

Destiny Woman

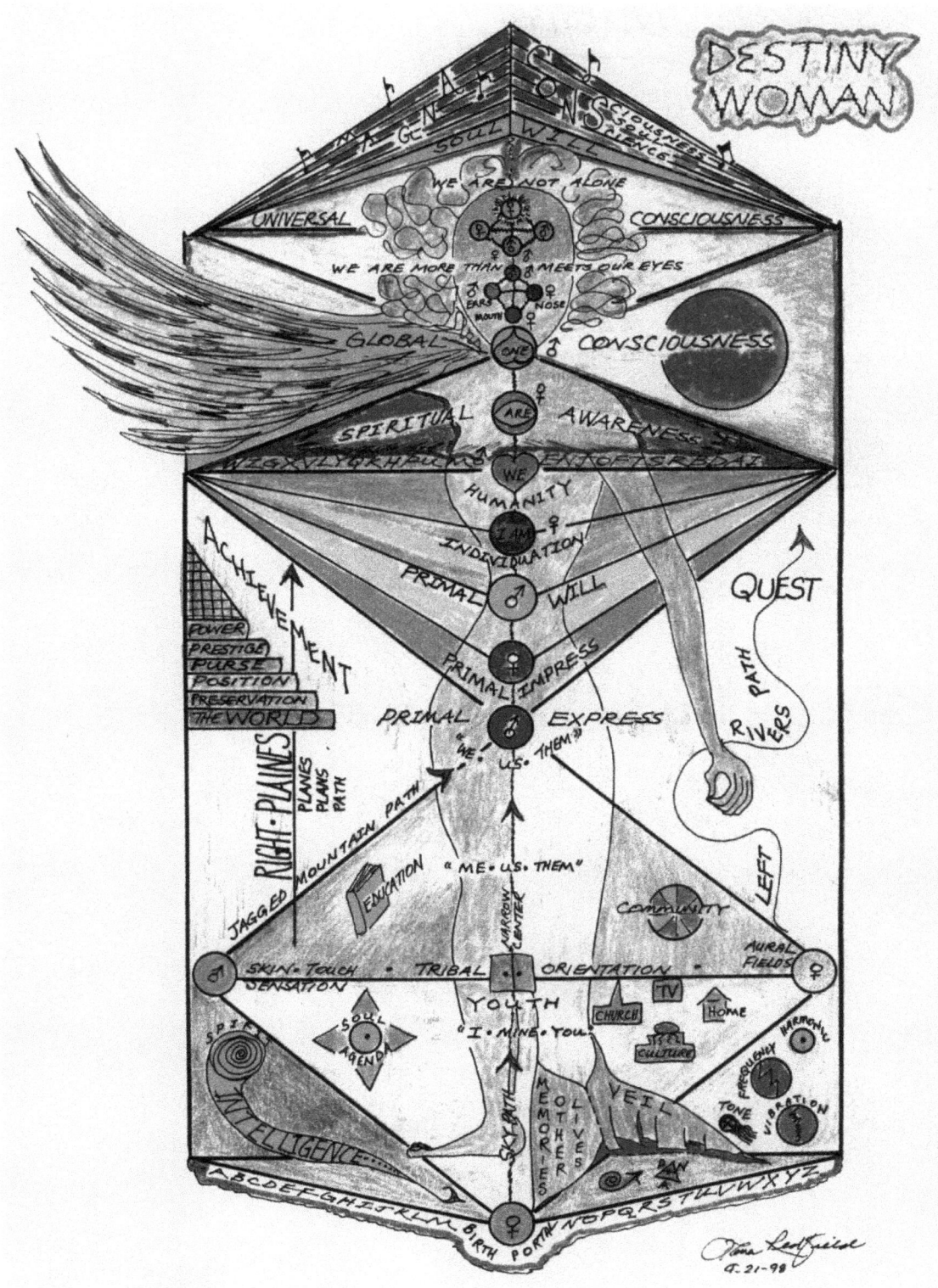

Fairchild

This is a pictorial exploration of certain ideas.

All of these drawings were inspired by working with the Alphabet.

Appendix: Other materials

Fairchild

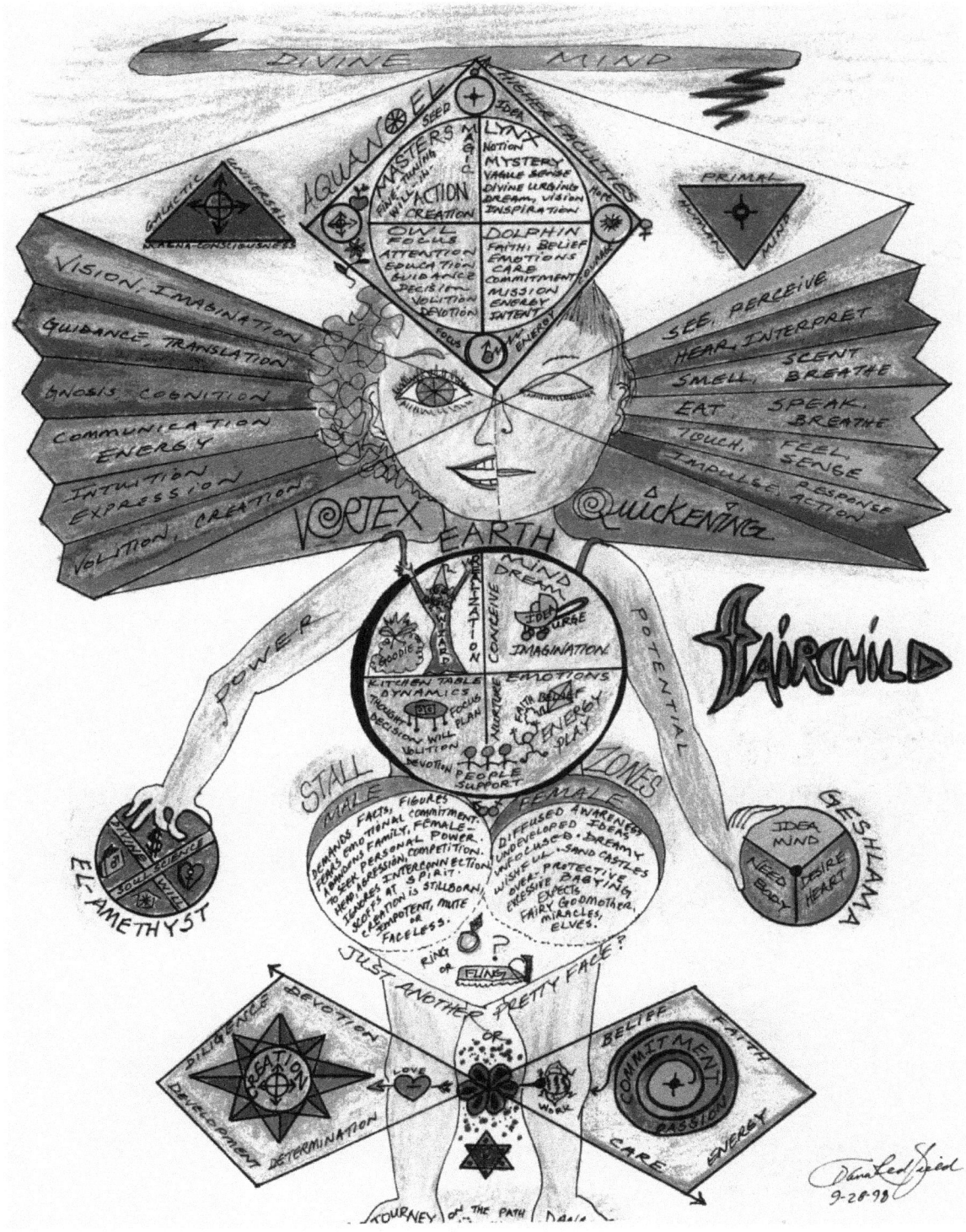

Humaniel

This drawing symbolizes man's journey of evolution of mind, body and spirit.

Appendix: Other materials

Humaniel

Alphabet Tree

On this page are several tools:

- The cipher
- The number totem pole,
- The House of Life.

The crystal script, the letter tree and the Sirius-Pleiades signet are my creations. The others were given to me by Guides.

Alphabet Tree

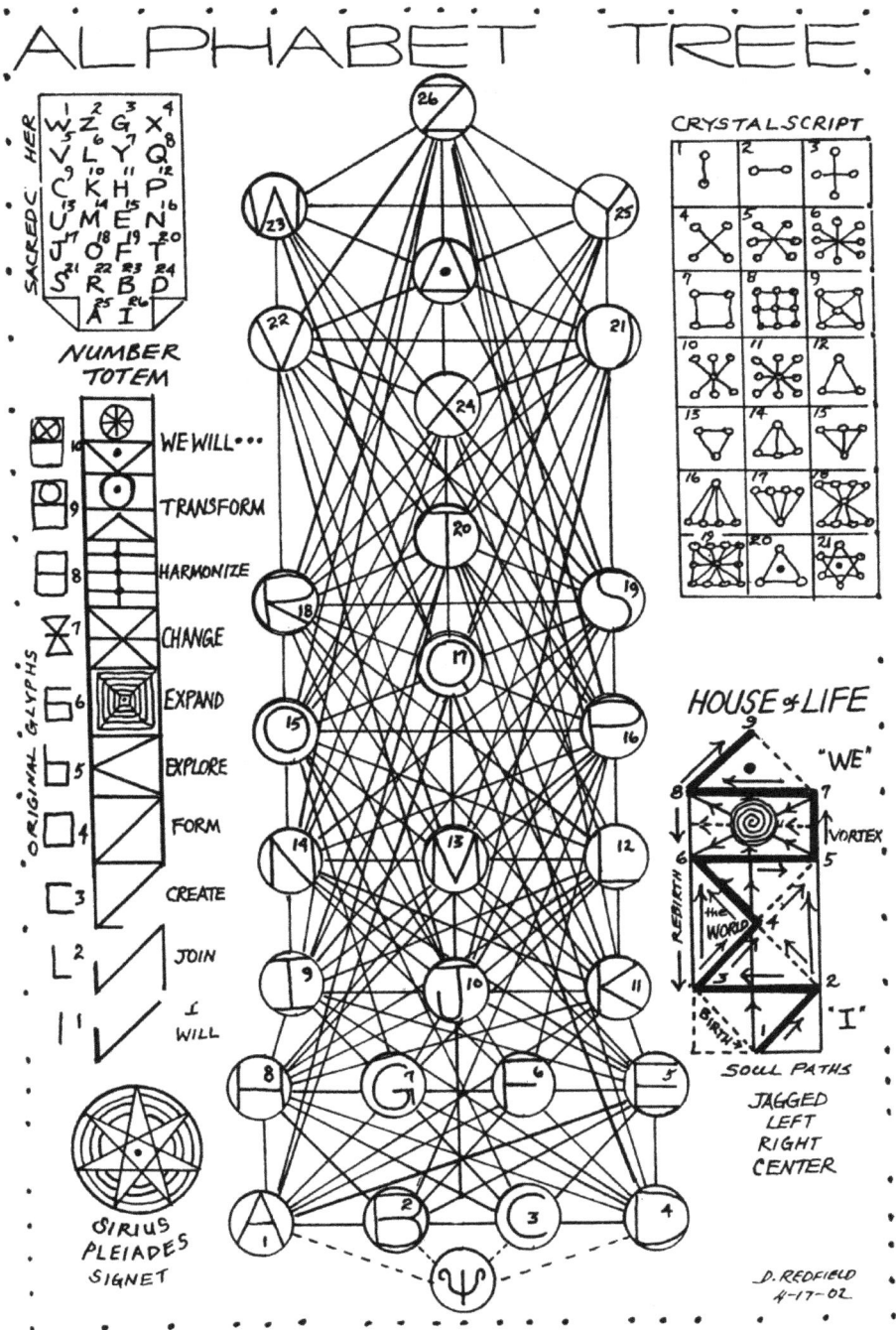

Three Letter Charts

The following are three letter charts that show the history of all of the letters, from the Egyptian of 3000 B.C. to Modern English.

I am unable to ink in the second chart now.

(Editor's Note: Melissa Black has inked in that chart where the lettering was faint.)

The third chart helped me in the study of the development of letters across the ages. It shows that there are missing links in the histories that I found in reference books.

These, like everything else in the Appendices, are included in the book "for the record." They are complicated and obscure.

(Editor's Note: Dana Redfield was concerned that these drawings may not be worthy of inclusion in the book. However, I felt that her thoughts deserved their place, perhaps acting as a springboard for further work by others.)

APPENDIX: OTHER MATERIALS

Three Letter Charts

		Egyptian 3000 B.C.	Semetic 1500 B.C.	Phoenician 1000 B.C.	Greek 600 B.C.	Etruscan	Roman	Medieval
Egyptian (Hebrew) A	Ox Head (Aleph)							
See R / B	House (Bet)							
See G / C	(Originally G – C added in Rome) →							
D	Door (Dalet)							
See H (He)(Hey) / E	Man Rejoicing							
F	Same as U, V, W and Y until ...							
(Z was herb) G	Throwing Stick (Gimel)(Camel)							
(Fence)(Knotted Rope) CH TH (Cheth)(Teth)								
H (Heth)(Window)								
See Z / I J	Hand (Yod) / (Added in Rome) →							
K	Cupped Hand (Kaph)							
See C, G ? P ? / L	Goad, Staff (Lamed)							
M	Water (Mem)							
N	Snake (Nun)							
Samech (Shelter) → O	Eye (Ayin)							
See C / P	Mouth (Peh)							
(Back of Head) Q	Monkey (Qoph)							
R	Head (Resh)							
(SH) S	Tooth (Shin)							
(See Tz and X) T	Mark (Tav)							
(Tz) (Tzadi)	(See X below)							
U W Y V (Rome)	Tent Hook (Vav)							
(See Tz and T) X	Fish							
See I / Z	Arrow, Weapon (Zayin)							

Appendix: Other materials

Three Letter Charts

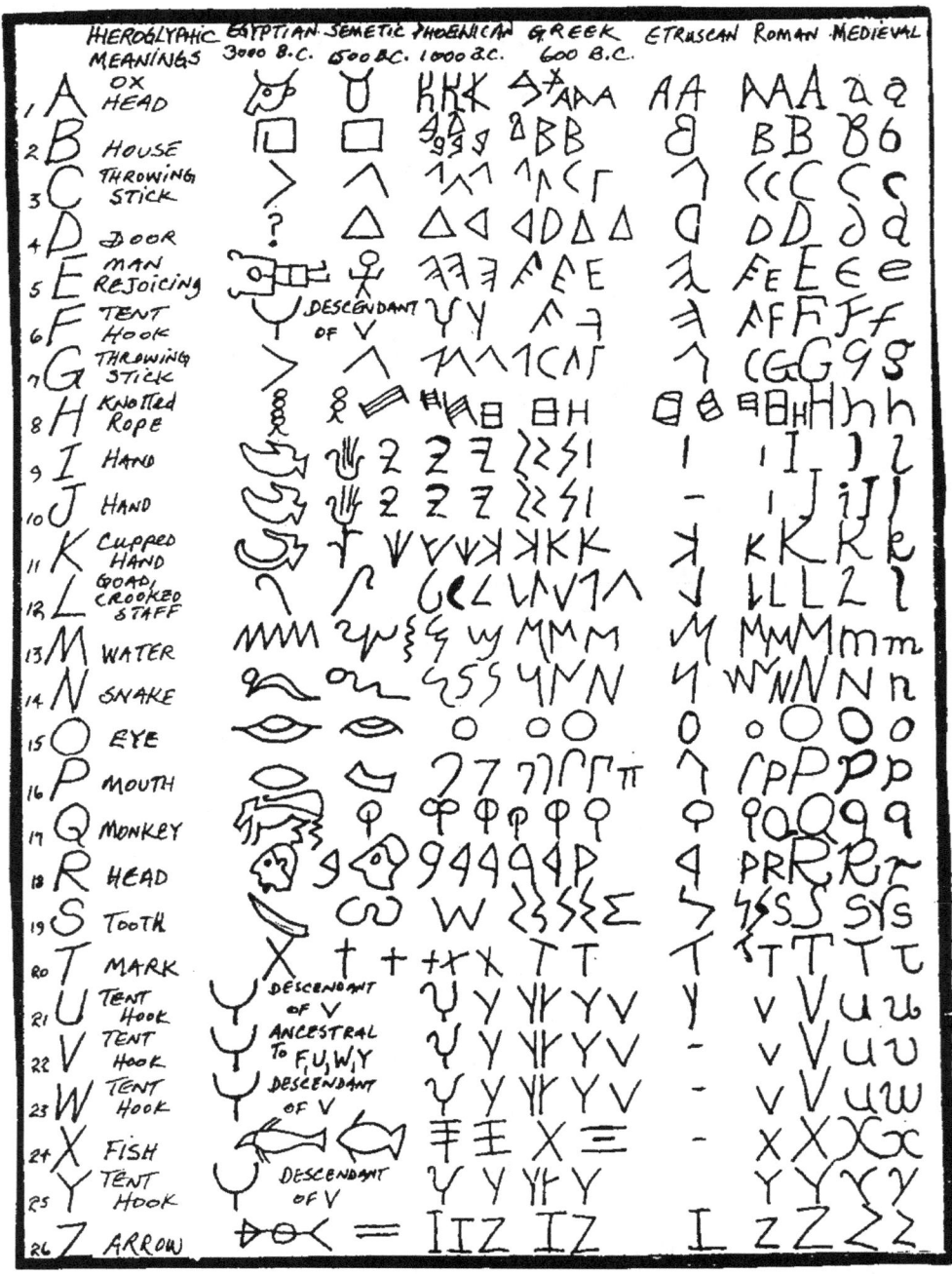

Appendix: Other materials

Three Letter Charts

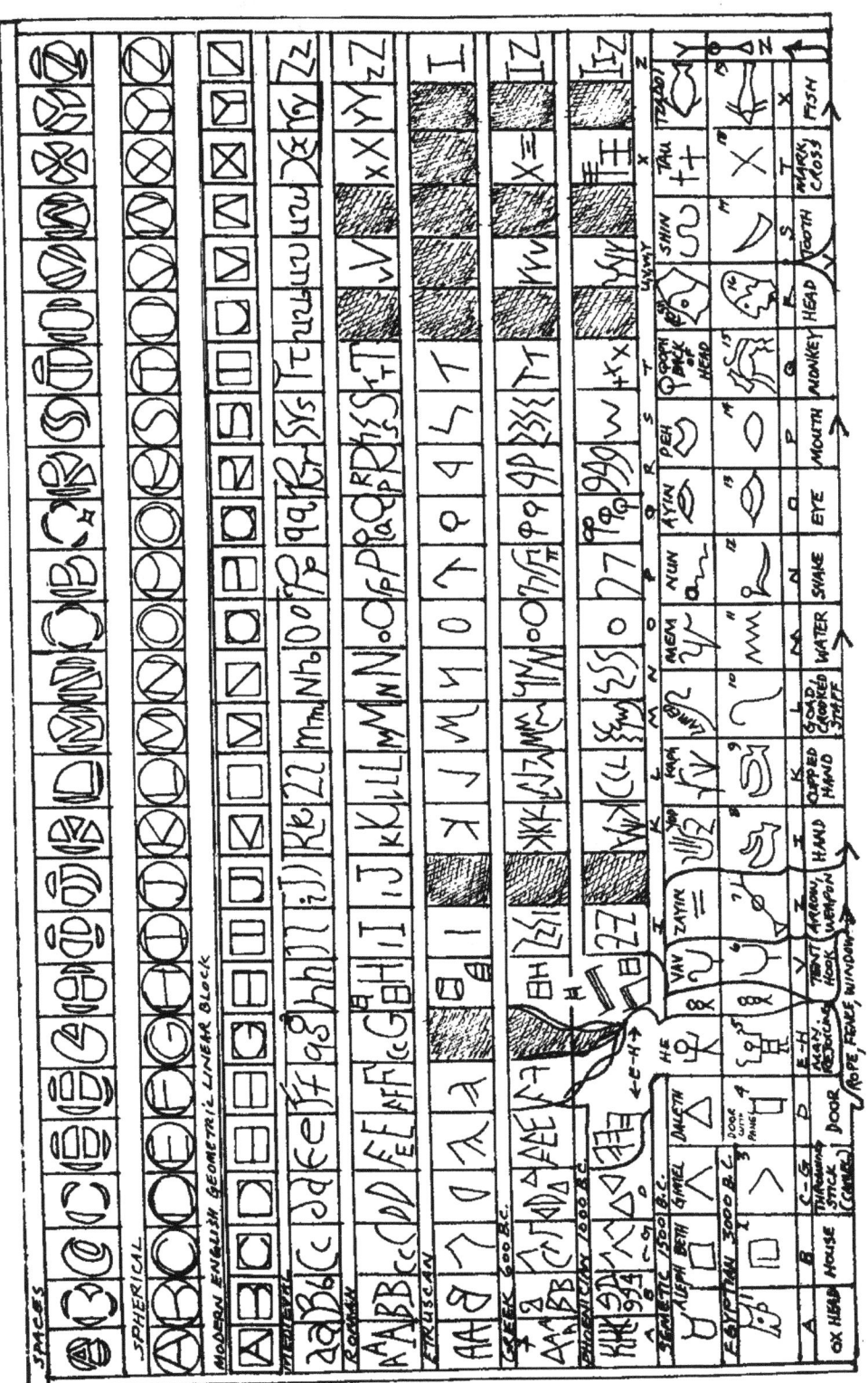

The House of Life

This structure came to me in a dream. As soon as I awakened I sketched what I could recall, and immediately began the work of discovering the mystery and purpose behind it.

Later I realized that it was similar to the Hebrew Tree of Life.

The House appears in several of the letter Mosaics.

Appendix: Other materials

The House of Life

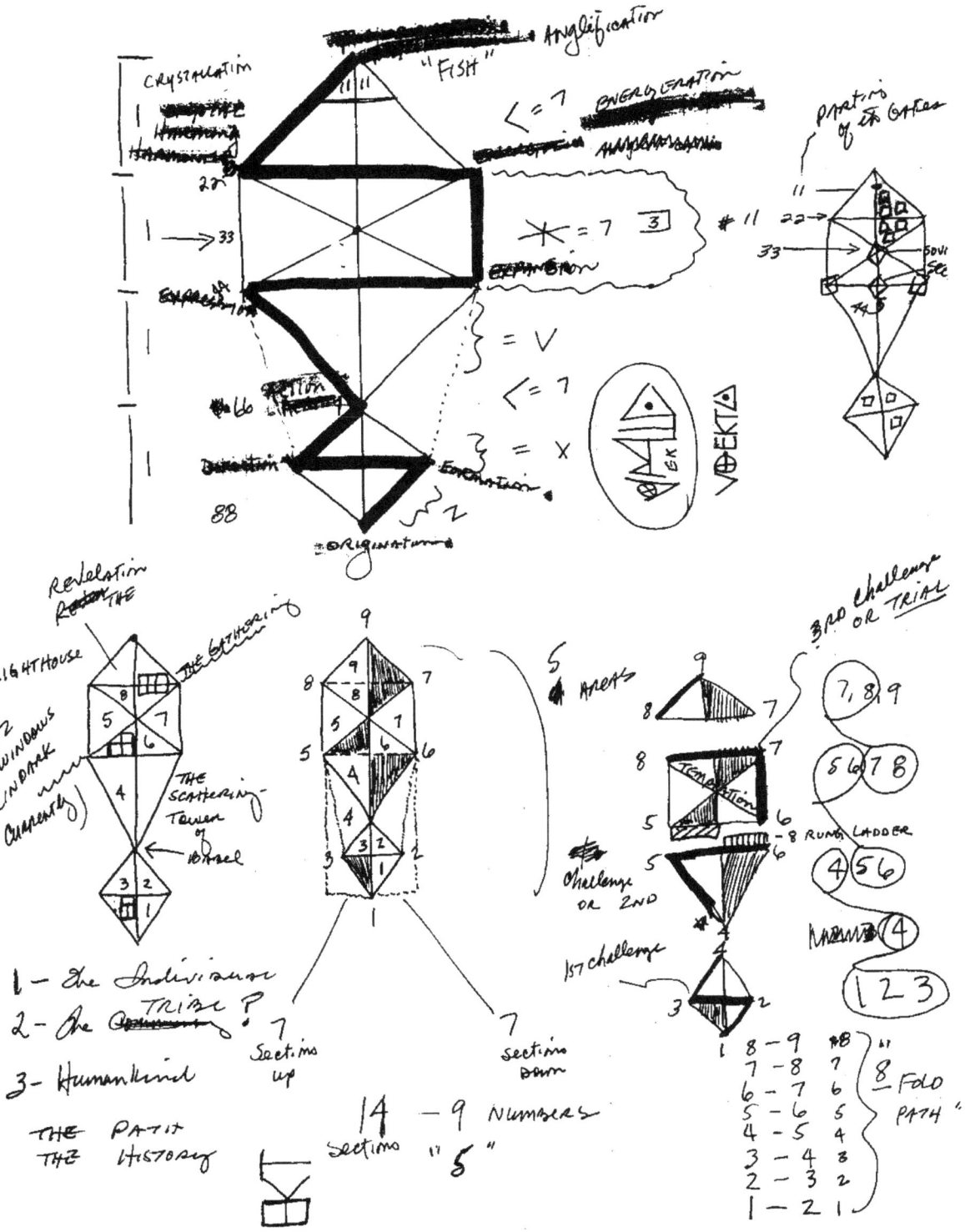

Crossing the T-Gate into the Arch of Infinity

Here is something else "for the record." At the time of its creation it was deeply significant to me. Unfortunately I did not retain conscious knowledge of the meanings. The experience is stamped in my house of memory somewhere, I feel certain.

I do recall that this picture has something to do with the Golden Mean of sacred geometry.

The key was in the fact that in our alphabet, the letter T is number 20. This letter is also number 20 in the cipher given to me. T is the only letter that is in the same numerical position in both alphabet orders.

(Editor's Note: The Golden Mean or Golden Section is represented by the Greek Letter phi. The origin of the Golden Mean is lost in antiquity. The decimal representation of phi is 1.6180339887499 and so on to infinity.

This ratio appears regularly in series that grow in steps. One example is the Fibonacci series, which is devised from adding the previous two numbers to make a new number. The Fibonacci series goes 0, 1, 1, 2, 3, 5, 8, 13, 21, 34, 55, 89, 144, and on to infinity.

This series can be found in living things. The Nautilus shell, for example, grows at the rate of phi. The sunflower has 55 clockwise spirals, which are overlaid by either 34 or 89 counterclockwise spirals, which is a phi proportion also.)

Crossing the T-Gate into the Arch of Infinity

CROSSING the T-GATE into the ARCH of INFINITY

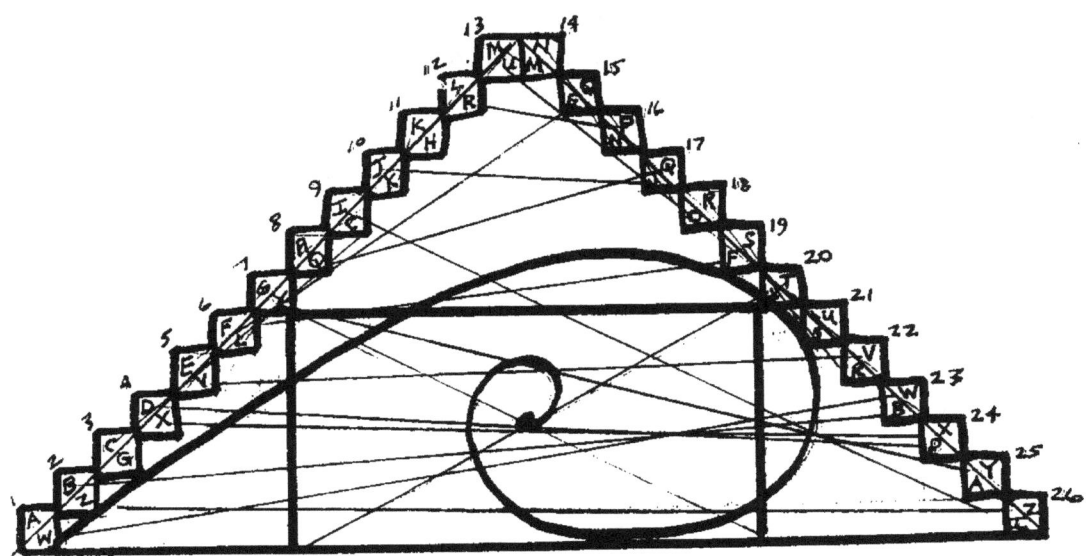

Hebrew Letters by Toby and Edelson

Elihu Edelson, who found the font for the Wisdoms for the Mosaics, and helped me assemble them, also sent me a wonderful guide by L. F. Toby for writing the Hebrew letters. Eli also sent me a table he made for my study and use.

(Editor's Note: The guide is titled The Art of Hebrew Lettering. *It was published by Phillip Feldheim Publishers and was copyrighted in 1985 and 2002.)*

Appendix: Other materials

Hebrew Letters by Toby and Edelson

א	⊀	Aleph	1	Ox		ל	L	Lamed	30	Ox Goad
ב	⊃	Beth	2	House	600 מ	ש	Mem	40	Water
ג	↗	Gimel	3	Camel	נ	ע	Nun	50	Fish
ד	⊲	Daleth	4	Door	700 ס	₮	Samekh	60	Prop
ה	⊒	Heh	5	Window	ע	O	Ayin	70	Eye
ו	Y	Vav	6	Nail, Hook	פ 800	⌐	Peh	80	Mouth
ז	I	Zayin	7	Sword Weapon	צ	⊢	Tzaddi	90	Fish Hook
ח	⊞	Cheth	8	Fence	900 ק	⊕	Qoph	100	Back of Head
ט	⊗	Teth	9	Serpent	ר	◁	Resh	200	Head
י	ꙅ	Yod	10	Hand	ש	W	Shin	300	Tooth
ך כ	Ψ	Kaph	20	Hand (palm)	ת	X	Tav	400	Mark, Cross

500 REDIS ALPHABET BY L.F. TOBY   TABLE BY ELIHU EDELSON

Appendix: Other materials

Master Sheet for the Letters

This was my original master sheet for the study of the letters of the Alphabet. As soon as I became aware of the dictate, "I want to know every letter of the Alphabet intimately," I began to picture them all as three-dimensional geometric structures. Key words that best touch on each letter's essence and energies emerged with time and study.

(Editor's Note: I never found Dana's original chart. The existing chart, a copy of a copy, was almost entirely illegible to the naked eye. This chart was reconstructed and re-inked by Melissa Black.)

Appendix: Other materials

Master Sheet for the Letters

Appendix: Other materials

Master Sheet for the Letters

OX HEAD / ARCHER

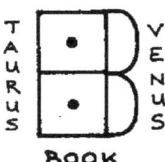

HOUSE / BOOK

THROWING STICK / CHALICE

ASCEND	BELIEF	CEREMONY
ACTIVATE	BLUEPRINT	COORDINATE
ASTROLOGY	BUILD	CREATE
ADAM	BEGIN	CRYSTAL
ARCHETYPE	BORN	CARE
ANGEL	BE	CYCLE
ATTRIBUTE	BEAUTY	CHERISH
ADORE	BASE	CHILD
ANGLE	BOX	CIRCULATE
ASPECT	BEE	CIPHER
AMBASSADOR	BULL	COMPASS
	BRIDGE	COMMUNITY
		CHORUS
		CELESTIAL
		ALCHEMY

Master Sheet for the Letters

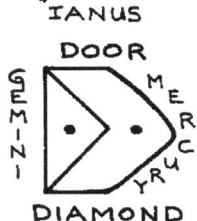
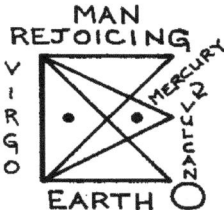

DIAMOND	EARTH	FLAME
DUALITY	ESSENCE	FORESIGHT
DEMONSTRATE	ENERGIZE	FUSION
DOMINION	EAST	FORT
DIVINE	EGYPTIAN	FORM
DESTINY	ESOTERIC	FLOWER
DNA	EVOLUTION	FEAST
DYNASTY	ETERNAL	FLAMINGO
DRUM	ENVIRONMENTAL	FOUNTAIN
DANCE	EIGHT	FABRIC
DRAMA		FANTASY
DREAM		FEY
DIMENSION		FLAVOR

* Roman God Ianus – Presided over doorways (his two faces let him see IN/OUT) as a sort of Celestial Janitor. January (Janos) marks going in, coming out.

Master Sheet for the Letters

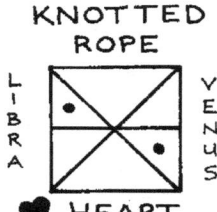
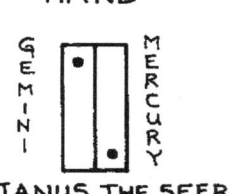

THROWING STICK	KNOTTED ROPE	HAND
GATEKEEPER (Capricorn / Saturn)	HEART (Libra / Venus)	IANUS, THE SEER (Gemini / Mercury)
GUARD	HOLOGRAPHIC	INTUITION
GESTATE	HARMONIZE	INTEGRATE
GOVERN	HOROSCOPE	IDEA
GLOBE	HIERARCHY	IMAGINATION
GALAXY	HEAVEN	INFORMATION
GRAND	HONEY	ILLUMINATION
GIVE	HUMAN	INDIVIDUAL
GROUND	HERALD	ISLAND
GESTALT	HOPE	INTEGER
GOLD	HATCH	ILLUSION
GROW	HARNESS	INFANT
GRASP	HOLD	IDIOT
GLEAN	HERMIT	IDOL
	HERD	IMP
		ID

Master Sheet for the Letters

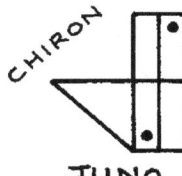 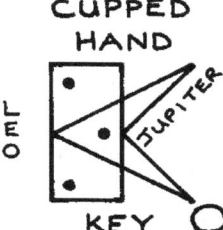 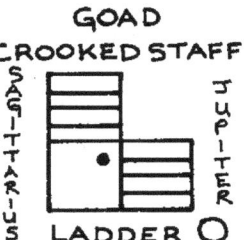

JOIN	KINGDOM	LAW
JOY	KNOWLEDGE	LIGHT
JUXTAPOSE	KINDLE	LEFT
JESTER	KILN	LOGIC
JOKER	KINETIC	LEVEL
JOUST	KNIGHT	LIMIT
JUBILANT	KEEN	LUCID
JUDGE	KALEIDESCOPE	LIFE
JUDAS	KIN	LOVE
JURY	KEN	LIKENESS
JELL	KINDRED	LOOM
JINX	KIND	LEAD
	KARMA	LEGION
		LITERATURE
		LITERAL
		LUXURY

Master Sheet for the Letters

WATER	SNAKE	EYE
CANCER / MOON	PISCES / NEPTUNE	CAPRICORN / SATURN
MOON	NAVIGATER	ORGANIST

MOTH	NETHER WORLD	OSMOSIS
MAIDEN	NAME	ORCHESTRATE
MIRROR	NUMBER	ORBIT
MERCY	NET	OMNISCIENCE
METAPHOR	NORTH	ONE
MYSTIC	NINE	WHOLE – HOLE
MASS	NURTURE	ORACLE
MOVEMENT	NOETIC	OCTAVE
MANKIND	NOEL	OBSERVE
MAKE	NOSTALGIA	OVER
MOLD	NURSE	OUT
MIND	NORM	ORGANIZED
MIGHT	NEW	OASIS
MIRACLE	NOMAD	OVUM
MAINTAIN	NIGHT	OVAL
MYTH	NOBLE	ORIGINAL
MAGIC	NEXUS	OSCILLATE
MESSENGER	NUCLEAR	ORNATE
MACHINE		OTHER
		ORATOR
		ORBIT
		OMEN
		ORAL

Master Sheet for the Letters

MOUTH

LEO
JUPITER

PROFESSOR

PARADIGM
PATTERN
PEOPLE
PHYSICS
PARADOX
PRINCIPLE
POWER
PSYCHOLOGY
PARABLE
PEARL
PEACE

MONKEY

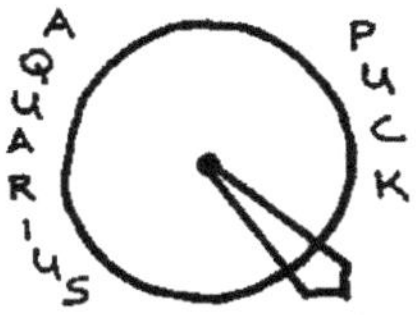
AQUARIUS
PUCK

QUESTER

QUINTESSENCE
QUALITY
QUICKEN
QUIRK
QUEEN
QUEST
QUOTA
QUARREL
QUELL
QUAKE
QUICKSILVER
QUINTA

HEAD

ARIES
MARS

RAINBOW

REASON
REVERBERATE
RAISE
RADAR
REALITY
RATIONAL
RIGHT
ROOT
RELIGION
RUDIMENT
ROCKET
RULE
ROTE
ROBOT
REASON

Master Sheet for the Letters

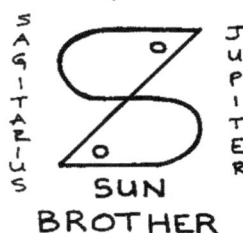

TUSK, TOOTH
SAGITTARIUS / JUPITER
SUN
BROTHER

MARK
TAURUS / VENUS
TRUMPET

TENT HOOK
VIRGO / VULCAN / MERCURY
UMBRELLA

SYNCHRONIZE	TIME	UTOPIA
SYMBOL	TRANSMIT	UPLIFT
SCRIBE	THINE	UNIVERSAL
SPIRIT	TOWER	UPSET
SOUL	TRUTH	URGENT
SACRED	TESTAMENT	UNCLE
STONE	THRONE	UNKNOWN
SPEAR	TRIUMPH	URN
SPELL	TABLOID	ULTIMATE
SPECTRUM	TURN	ULYSSES
SERPENT	TRUST	UNDERSTAND
SERVANT		UNDULATE
SIN		
SCROLL		
STAFF		
SEED		
SCHOLAR		
STAR		
SOUTH		

Appendix: Other materials

Master Sheet for the Letters

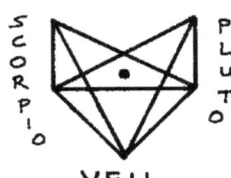
TENT HOOK
VEIL

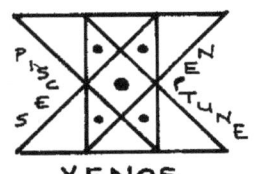
FISH
XENOS

WIZARD

VEIL	WIZARD	XENOS
VORTEX	WORD	EXALT
VIBRATE	WHEEL	EXPRESS
VALVE	WHIRLWIND	ALL NAMES
VIRTUE	WITCH	X FACTOR
VOLT	WILL	EXONERATE
VENT	WISDOM	EXIT
VIGOR	WORK	EXIST
VICTORY	WEST	AXIS
VAPOR	WATER	EXOTIC
VALIDATE	WAVE	EXILE
VAULT	WHALE	EXTRATERRESTRIAL
VEGABOND	WAND	
VOYAGE	WONDER	
VITAL FORCE	WORLD	
VIPER	WEAVE	
VOODOO	WHEAT	
VISION	WORTH	
VOICE		
VARY		
VEER		
VERTIGO		
VALENTINE		
VALIANT		
VAGUE		
VESSEL		
VENTURE		
VIS VITALIS		
VITALITY		
LIVING FORCE		
VITAL FORCE		
WALK THE EARTH		

Appendix: Other materials

Master Sheet for the Letters

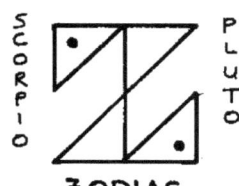

YIN	ZEN
YEARN	ZEAL
YIELD	ZION
TREE OF LIFE	ZIGOTE
YOLK	ZEST
YOKE	ZOOM
YORE	ZOO
YOGI	ZEPHER
YOUNG	ZONE
YAW	ZENITH

Set I: Five Compound Drawings

Here begins 5 sets of drawings. I began with "compounds," receiving visions of images for particular combinations of two letters.

The drawings are rough because I never dreamed I would be copying them to be considered for inclusion in a book. The whole project became overwhelming over the years. Redrawing any of the beginning pictures and tools became impossible. These are all "for the record." They belong to the whole of my work to know the letters of the alphabet intimately.

APPENDIX: OTHER MATERIALS

Set I: Five Compound Drawings

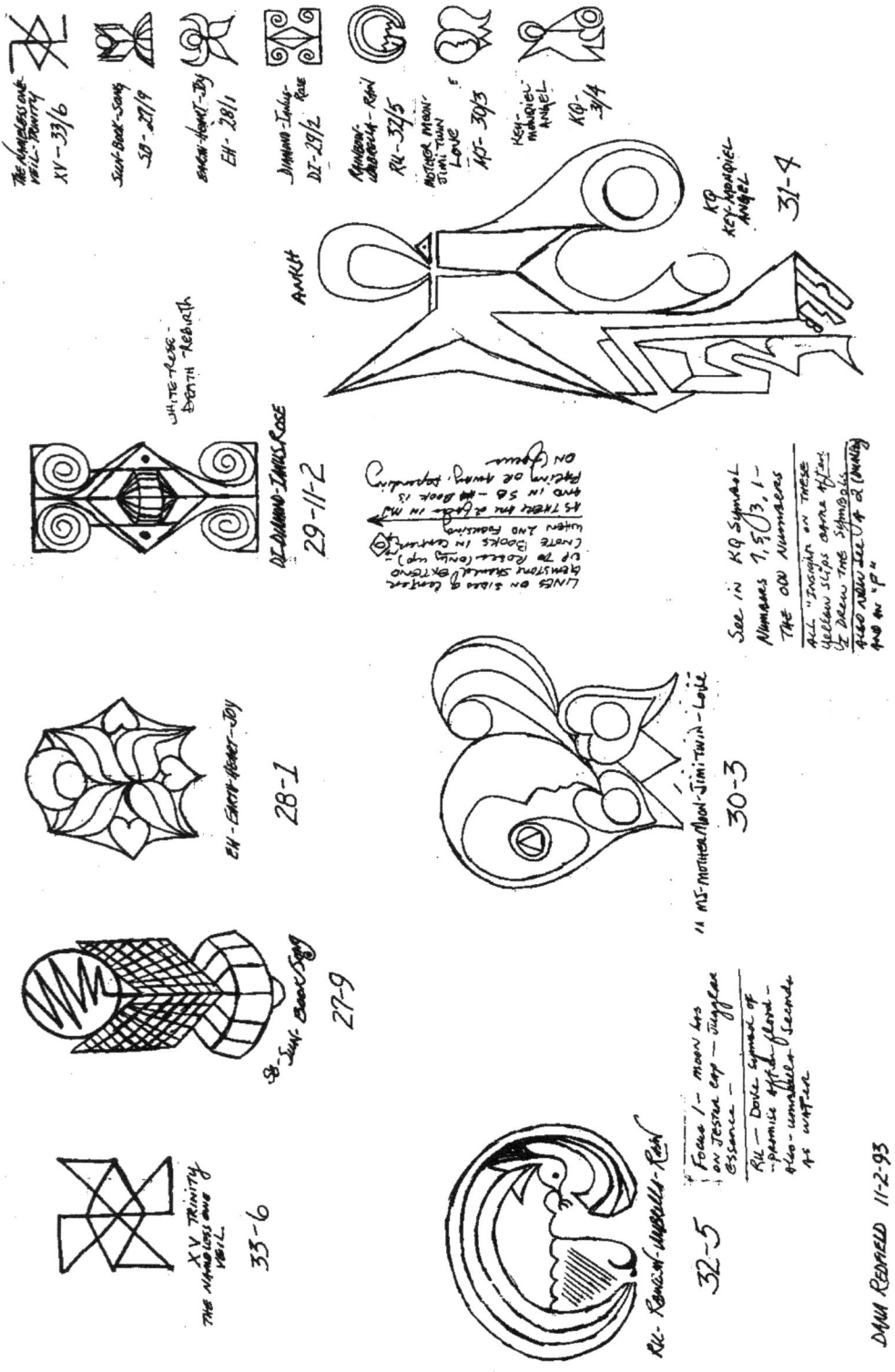

Set II: Six Compound Drawings

Set II consists of more complex drawings of specific compounds, each consisting of 2 letters. There are six drawings in Set II.

When I was doing these drawings I was in an altered state of mind, and at times I felt that guides, or some power, were moving my hand. I could never draw like this before, and have been unable to draw this well since.

Appendix: Other materials

Set II: Six Compound Drawings

Appendix: Other materials

Set II: Six Compound Drawings

Set II: Six Compound Drawings

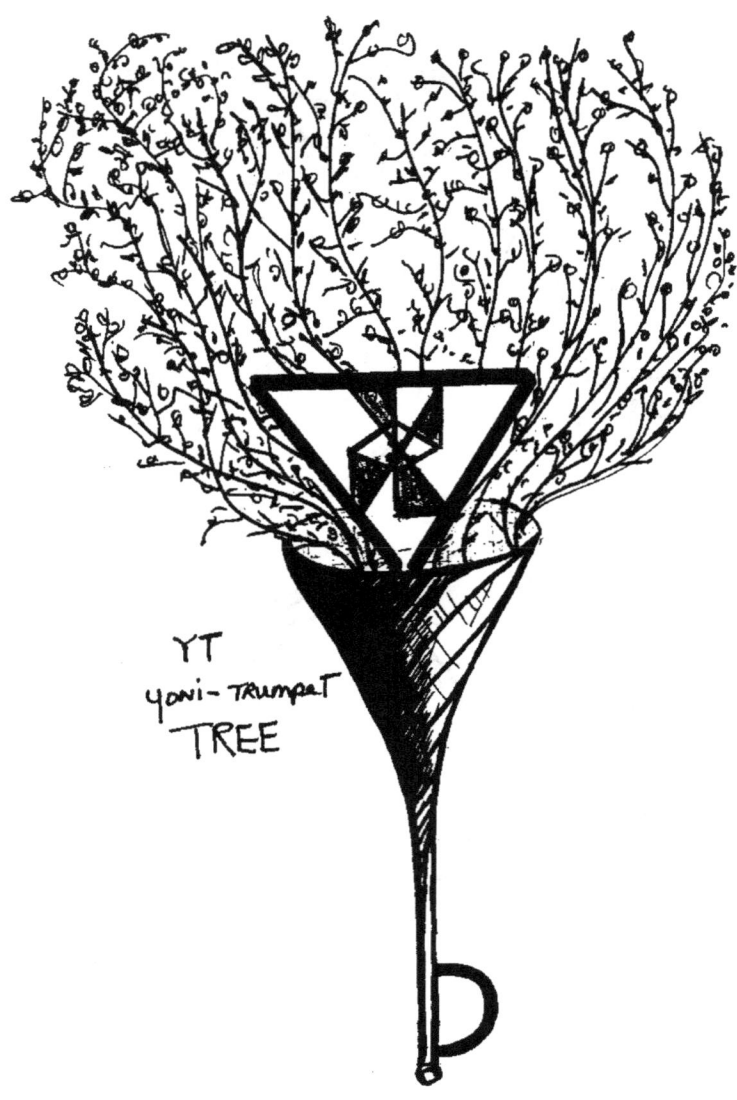

Set II: Six Compound Drawings

GC – BRIDE
GATEKEEPER – CHALICE

Set II: Six Compound Drawings

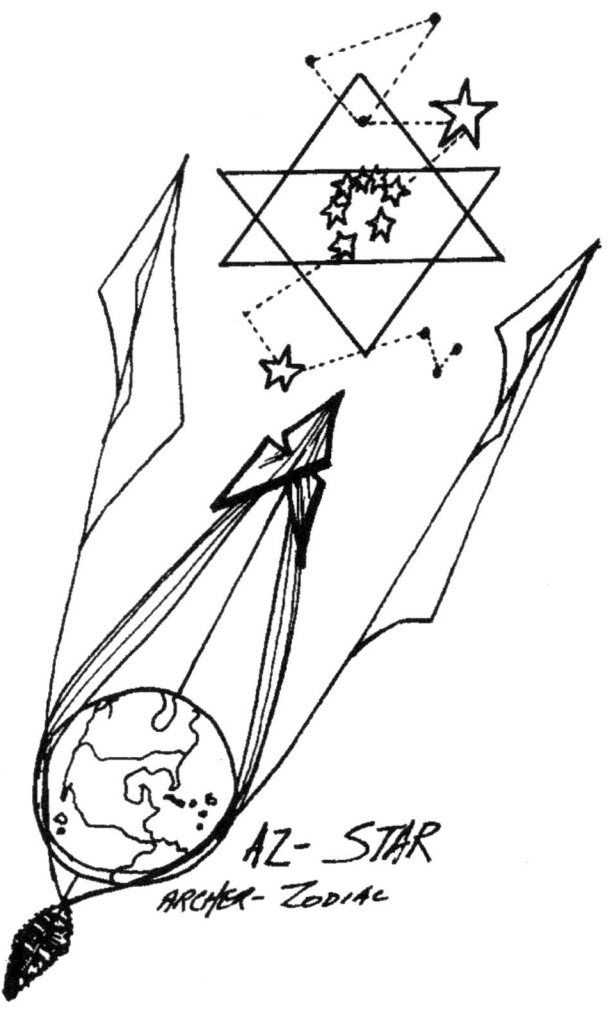

Appendix: Other materials

Set II: Six Compound Drawings

Set III: Six Compound Drawings

Set III consists of 6 drawings. They are much more complicated than Set II. Understandings given to me about the Twelve Tribes of Israel were incorporated in these drawings, along with other ideas I've long since forgotten.

Some of the images in this set are in some of the Mosaics. For instance, "Storming the Gates" appears on the "I" Mosaic page.

Set III: Six Compound Drawings

Appendix: Other materials

Set III: Six Compound Drawings

Appendix: Other materials

Set III: Six Compound Drawings

Appendix: Other materials

Set III: Six Compound Drawings

Set III: Six Compound Drawings

Appendix: Other materials

Set III: Six Compound Drawings

Set IV: Drawings with Larger Concepts

The drawings in Set IV represent larger concepts.

The sayings, such as "It's the thought that counts," which is added to the first drawing, came after the drawings were completed.

I had a kind of vision of the strange musical-note symbol in the half-awake, half-sleeping state. I remember getting up in the night to draw it.

I spent a lot of time getting the drawings in Set IV "right."

Appendix: Other materials

Set IV: Drawings with Larger Concepts

Appendix: Other materials

Set IV: Drawings with Larger Concepts

Appendix: Other materials

Set IV: Drawings with Larger Concepts

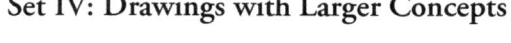

Burning Bridges

Appendix: Other materials

Set IV: Drawings with Larger Concepts

Appendix: Other materials

Set IV: Drawings with Larger Concepts

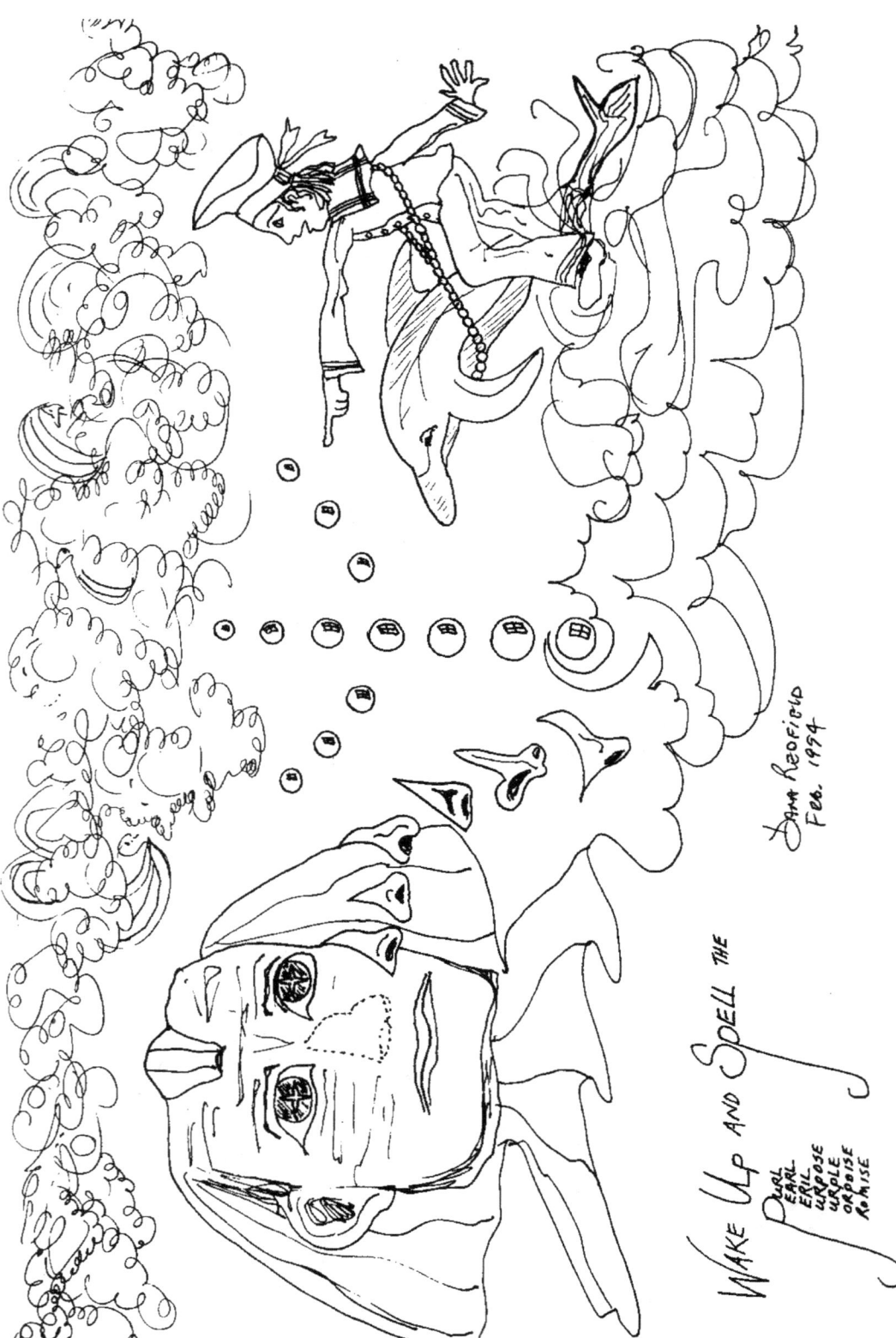

Appendix: Other materials

Set IV: Drawings with Larger Concepts

133

Set IV: Drawings with Larger Concepts

Set V: Abstractions

The drawings of Set V came as abstractions. There was supposed to be a message for each, but after the first message, I fell ill and the window for completing the set, images and messages passed.

Set V: Abstractions

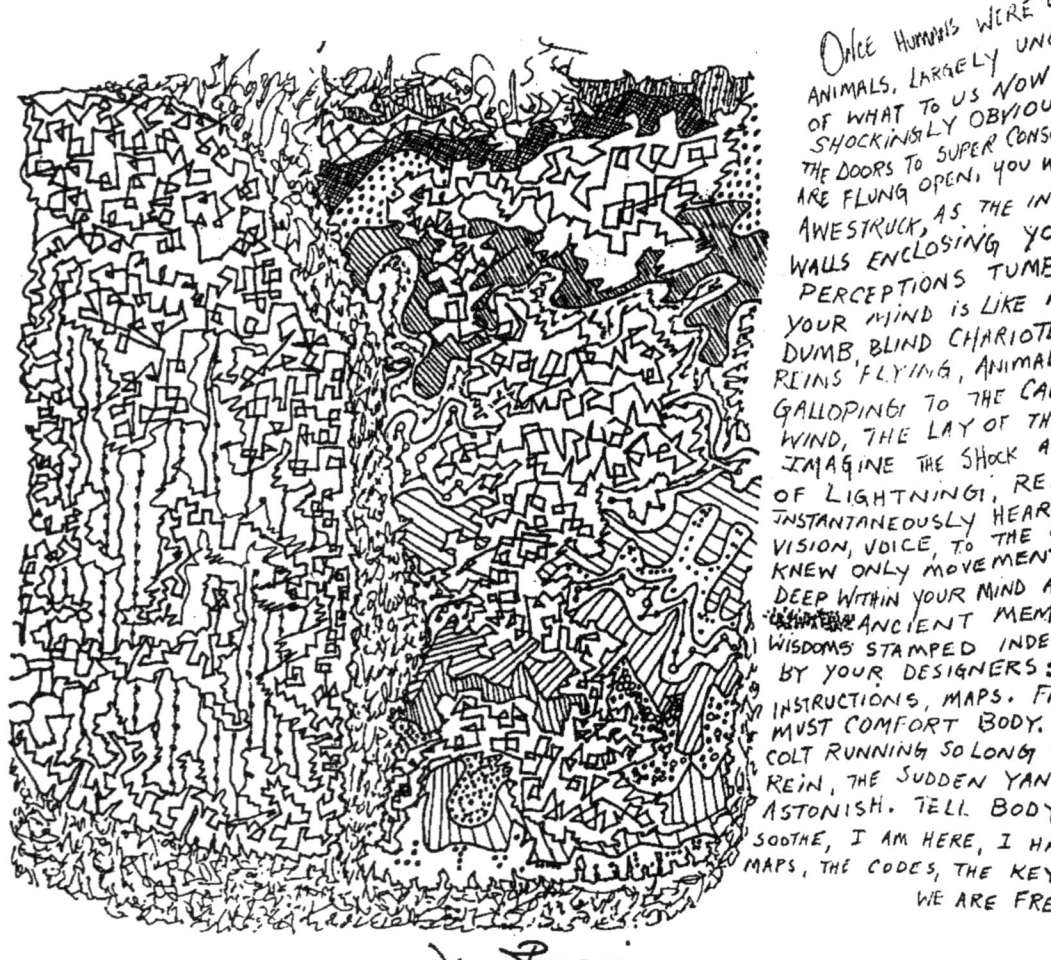

Once humans were like animals, largely unconcious of what to us now seems shockingly obvious. When the doors to super consciousness are flung open, you will tremble, awestruck, as the invisible walls enclosing your perceptions tumble. Your mind is like a deaf, dumb, blind charioteer, reins flying, animal beneath galloping to the call of the wind, the lay of the land. Imagine the shock as a bolt of lightning, restoring, instantaneously hearing, vision, voice, to the one who knew only movement. Fear not. Deep within your mind are >>> ancient memories, wisdoms stamped indelibly by your designers: codes, instructions, maps. First you must comfort body. Like the colt running so long free of rein, the sudden yank will astonish. Tell body, soothe soothe, I am here, I have the maps, the codes, the keys.
  We are free now.

Dana Redfield
12-93

Appendix: Other materials

Set V: Abstractions

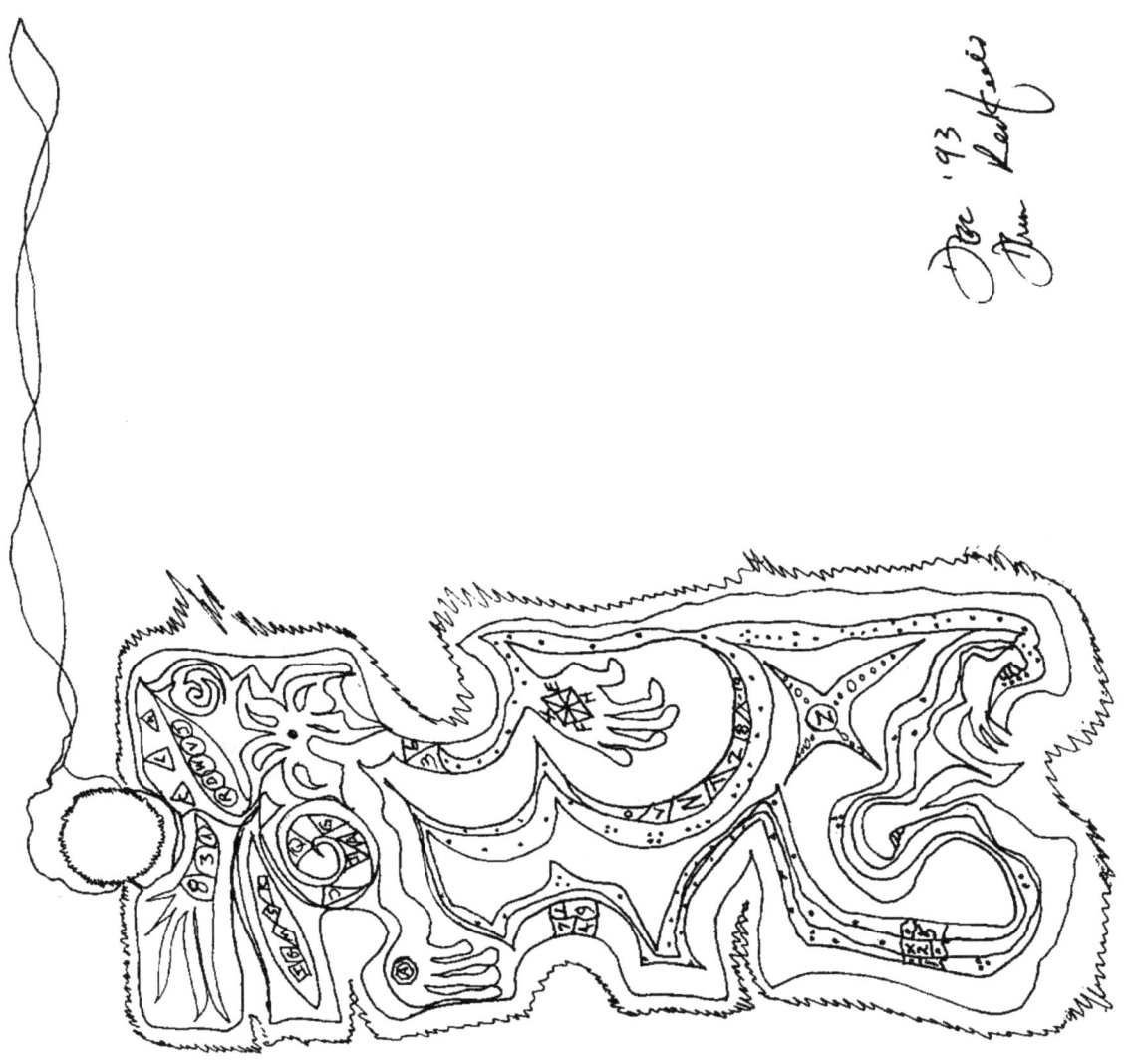

Set V: Abstractions

Appendix: Other materials

Set V: Abstractions

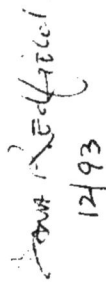

Appendix: Other materials

Set V: Abstractions

Unifying Principle

In January 1994, after intense work on the alphabet, the message below came to me. By then I understood that when I worked with the letters and numbers, doing work with Gematria and other inspired exercises, the result was often an alert and altered state of mind, where I could receive such information.

QBL—the root of the word Qabala—means "to receive." See the Q Mosaic.

Here is the message:

> All worlds are separate but connected, each unique and similar to other worlds. Worlds on a particular continuum most closely resemble other worlds on that continuum, all unique and separate and similar to worlds parallel on other continuums or other realities.
>
> In a process of unification, each continuum aligns with all other continuums, all looping back to the center, each and all combining into one that inserts, as one, through the center. At the point of insertion, all worlds explode and scatter, each beginning as a center, supporting multiple continuums, or realities, each supporting separate but connected worlds.
>
> The continuums of the "original" system loop back to insert through the center as one. Throwing off worlds, the one now explodes itself into an intricate pattern that constitutes a new octave of reality.
>
> So the evolution of persons occurs. The worlds that scatter to form new systems are offspring resulting from eons of development in multitudes of continuums, the essence of that multitudinous development splitting away from its offspring to experience a new octave of reality, symbolized in your mythology as immortality, personalized by separate individualities, or angels in Heaven.
>
> The nature of evolutions higher than those symbolically illustrated here within do not translate into words, images, feelings or thoughts.
>
> All is energy, sound, light, movement and design, never ending. All is unique, separate-and-connected, love personified in an infinitude of expression.

Unifying Principle

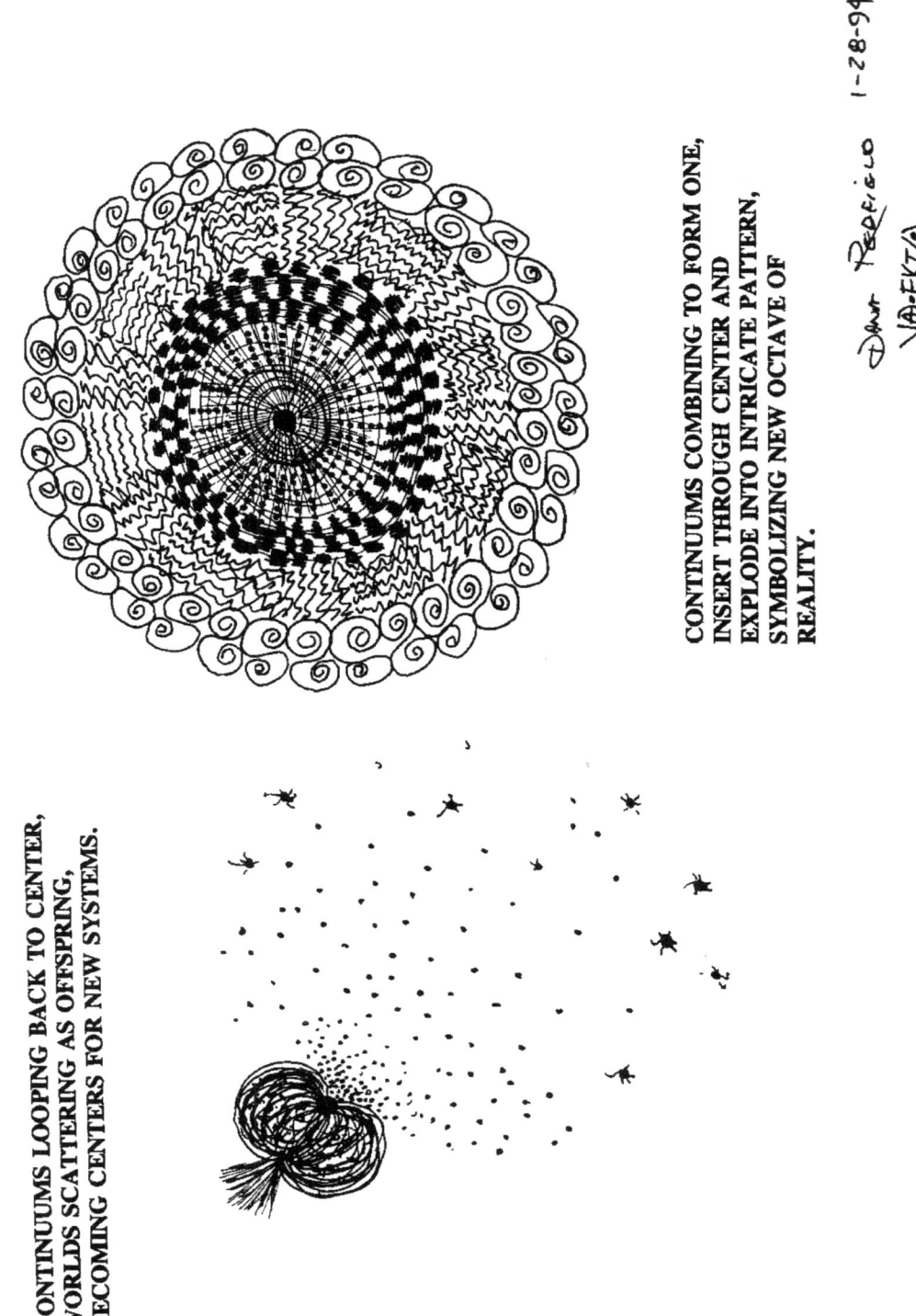

Unifying Principle

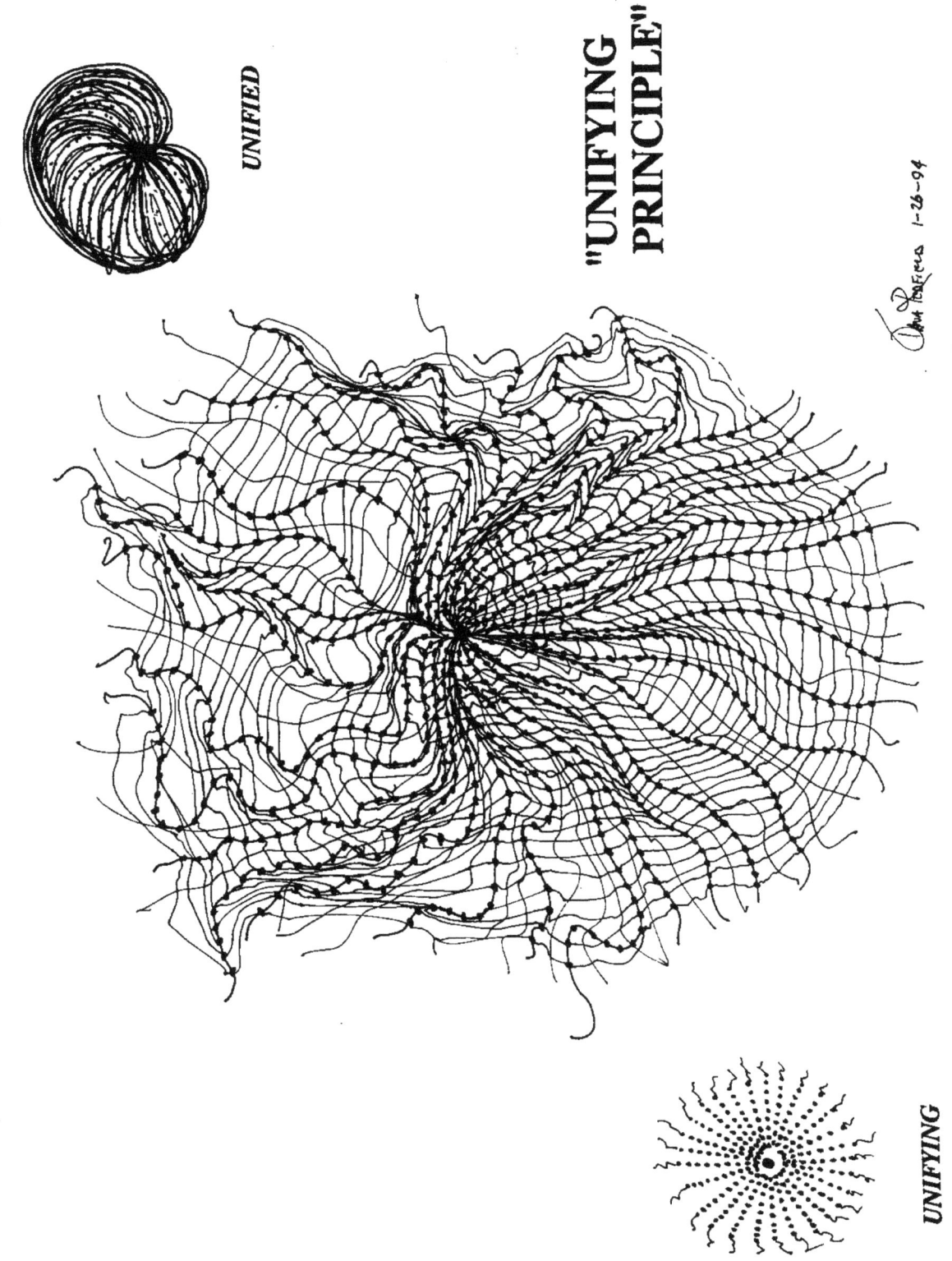

About the Author

Dana Morse Redfield was born on January 30, 1944, in Covina, California, the daughter of Yvonne Sorenson Morse and Nolan R. Morse. She was raised in Wyoming, Texas, Oklahoma and Utah. She attended Northeastern State College in Oklahoma and Brigham Young University in Utah. She is survived by one daughter, Michelle Yvonne Tomburello.

Her published works include three books of imaginative fiction, *Ezekiel's Chariot, Lucy Blue and the Daughters of Light* and *Jonah,* and two non-fiction books, *Summoned: Encounters with Alien Intelligence* and *The ET-Human Link: We Are the Message*.

For the last several years of her life, she resided in Moab, Utah and she died there, after a gallant struggle with several forms of cancer, on April 14, 2007. She willed to L/L Research three of her unpublished works, *All My Days Are Shadows of Tomorrow: An Autobiography,* the uncut version of *Jonah,* and this present work, *The Alphabet Mosaics,* which L/L Research is privileged to publish now. We hope to edit the remaining two works and publish them as e-books in the future as well.

She wrote very truly of herself in her obituary,

"She played some music, made some art,
Wrote some books, gave her heart."

www.ingramcontent.com/pod-product-compliance
Lightning Source LLC
Chambersburg PA
CBHW062131160426
43191CB00013B/2261